AI for Real Work

AI for Real Work

How to Think, Decide, and Build with AI

Saurabh Jaiswal

This book is intended for informational and educational purposes only. The author makes no representations or warranties regarding the completeness or accuracy of the contents. The strategies and concepts discussed are based on professional experience and are not a substitute for independent judgment or professional advice.

ISBN 978-93-5768-804-8
First Edition 2026

For my family, friends, mentors, and teachers—

and for the conversations that shaped how I think.

Life is a journey

It just goes on…

Table of Contents

List of Figures

List of Tables

Preface

I did not write this book because the world needs another explanation of artificial intelligence.

I wrote it because, over the past several years, I have seen a pattern repeat itself across organizations of different sizes, industries, and levels of technical maturity. The tools change. The terminology evolves. The excitement rises and falls. But the underlying confusion remains surprisingly consistent.

Artificial intelligence promises intelligence at scale. And in many cases, it delivers impressive technical capability. Yet again and again, I have watched capable teams struggle—not because they lacked skill, but because they lacked clarity.

Projects begin with enthusiasm and urgency. There is pressure to innovate, to keep up, to demonstrate capability. Proofs of concept are built. Dashboards are presented. Models show strong performance in controlled settings. For a moment, it feels like progress.

And then, something subtle happens.

The system does not quite integrate into daily work. Decision-makers hesitate. Ownership becomes unclear. Expectations drift. Trust erodes quietly. Eventually, the initiative slows or stalls—not dramatically, but gradually.

This is not a technical failure. It is a thinking failure.

In my experience working with Python and AI systems over the past decade and a half, I have learned that intelligence alone does not create value. What creates value is disciplined thinking around decisions. What problem are we truly solving? Which decision will change? Who owns that decision? What level of uncertainty is acceptable? How will trust be built and maintained?

These questions are rarely asked early enough.

There is also a deeper confusion surrounding AI adoption. Many organizations treat AI as a feature to be added, a capability to be integrated, or a competitive signal to be displayed. But AI is not a feature in the traditional sense. It is a system that introduces probabilistic behavior into environments that are often designed for certainty. It changes how decisions are made, who makes them, and how responsibility is understood.

That shift requires maturity.

Over time, I began to notice that the same mistakes appeared in different forms. Teams optimized technical performance without clarifying objectives. Leaders approved initiatives without defining ownership. Systems were scaled before trust was earned. Experiments were celebrated while production realities were underestimated.

None of this was caused by lack of intelligence. On the contrary, many of these teams were highly capable. The problem was not skill. It was sequence.

The sequence was wrong.

This book exists to restore that sequence.

It argues that decisions—not models—are the unit of value. It suggests that clarity reduces cost more effectively than optimization. It emphasizes that trust limits adoption more than accuracy. And it reminds us that responsibility does not disappear when a system becomes intelligent.

You will not find technical tutorials here. There are no algorithms explained, no code samples, no vendor comparisons. Those details are important in their place, but they are not the foundation of sustainable AI use. Foundations are built on thinking.

My intention in writing this book is not to slow down innovation. It is to strengthen it. When clarity comes first, complexity becomes manageable. When ownership is defined early, risk becomes navigable. When trust is treated as essential rather than assumed, adoption becomes stable.

AI is a powerful development in human capability. Used responsibly, it allows us to focus on higher-order judgment, creativity, and strategy. Used carelessly, it amplifies confusion and erodes confidence.

The difference lies in how we approach it.

If this book helps you ask better questions before building, define decisions more precisely, scale more responsibly, or say "not yet" with confidence when necessary, then it has served its purpose.

The world does not need more hype about artificial intelligence. It needs clearer thinking about how intelligence is applied.

That is what this book attempts to offer.

Introduction

Artificial intelligence is no longer a distant concept discussed only in research labs or technology conferences. It is already embedded in everyday work—shaping recommendations, prioritizing information, flagging risks, and influencing decisions across industries. Yet for all the activity and enthusiasm surrounding AI, one pattern remains consistent: many organizations struggle not because the technology is insufficient, but because the thinking around it is unclear.

This book was written to address that gap.

"AI for Real Work" is not about the latest tools, libraries, or breakthroughs. It is about how to think clearly when intelligence—artificial or human—enters a decision process. It is about discipline. It is about responsibility. And above all, it is about understanding that AI creates value only when it improves real decisions.

If you have ever seen an impressive demonstration that failed to translate into lasting impact, this book is for you. If you have witnessed a proof of concept that never became part of daily work, or a technically strong system that people did not trust, you have already encountered the challenges this book explores. These outcomes are rarely caused by code alone. More often, they result from unclear objectives, undefined ownership, unrealistic expectations, or weak alignment between systems and human behavior.

This book is written for business leaders who must evaluate AI initiatives without becoming technical specialists. It is written for technical professionals who want their systems to influence real outcomes, not just benchmarks. It is written for product teams navigating the transition from experimentation to production. It is written for executives considering how and when to scale AI responsibly. And it is written for consultants and advisors who help organizations think more clearly about technology adoption.

You do not need to be a data scientist to benefit from this book. You need only an interest in disciplined thinking and practical application.

Throughout these chapters, we will focus on a simple but often overlooked principle: decisions are the unit of value. Predictions, dashboards, and models may be impressive, but they are intermediate steps. The moment that matters is when a decision changes—when a resource is allocated differently, when a risk is handled earlier, when a process becomes more reliable, or when a strategy is refined.

By starting with decisions rather than tools, complexity becomes manageable. Objectives become sharper. Ownership becomes visible. And risk becomes something that can be designed for, rather than reacted to.

You will learn how to distinguish between tool-first thinking and decision-first thinking. You will see why proof-of-concept success often fails in production environments. You will understand why trust—not accuracy—often limits adoption. You will examine how scaling amplifies both strengths and weaknesses. And you will explore why long-term stewardship matters more than initial deployment.

You will also learn when not to use AI. Discipline includes restraint. Not every problem benefits from added intelligence, especially when objectives are unclear or ownership is undefined. Choosing not to automate a decision can be a mature, strategic choice.

This book is not a technical manual. You will not find code, formulas, or vendor comparisons here. Those details change rapidly. Principles do not.

If you are looking for model tutorials or tool walkthroughs, this is not that book. This book is about thinking clearly before you build.

The aim is to provide a way of thinking that remains useful even as tools evolve.

Technology will continue to advance. Systems will become more capable, faster, and more accessible. But certain fundamentals will remain steady. Organizations will still need clarity. Decisions will still carry consequences. Accountability will still be human. And trust will still take time to build.

If there is one theme that runs through these pages, it is that intelligence alone does not create value. Disciplined thinking does.

AI is powerful. It can analyze patterns at scale, surface insights quickly, and assist in complex environments. Used well, it allows people to focus on higher-order reasoning, creative work, and strategic judgment. Used carelessly, it amplifies confusion and erodes trust. The difference lies not in the technology itself, but in how thoughtfully it is applied.

As you read, you are invited to slow down your thinking—not to resist innovation, but to strengthen it. Ask clearer questions. Define decisions precisely. Identify ownership early. Design for trust. Plan for production. Scale with discipline. Commit to stewardship.

Throughout this book, I refer to this disciplined way of thinking as the **Decision-First AI Framework**. It is not a methodology or a checklist. It is a set of enduring principles:

- Define the decision before the system.
- Clarify ownership before automation.
- Design for trust, not just performance.
- Scale with responsibility.
- Treat AI as long-term stewardship, not a one-time deployment.

These principles are simple, but they are not easy. They require restraint, clarity, and patience. Yet they remain stable even as tools and capabilities evolve.

The goal of this book is not to make you more impressed by AI. It is to make you more deliberate in how you use it.

When intelligence enters a system, the standard for clarity rises. That is not a burden. It is an opportunity.

If you approach AI with structured thinking and steady responsibility, it becomes less mysterious and more manageable. It becomes a tool that supports human judgment rather than replacing it. And it becomes part of real work—not just experimentation.

The chapters that follow are an invitation to think differently about AI adoption. Not as a race to implement the latest capability, but as a disciplined effort to improve decisions over time.

Because in the end, AI does not create value by being intelligent. It creates value when we use intelligence—human and artificial—with clarity, ownership, and purpose.

Chapter 1
Rethinking Where AI Creates Value

The Illusion of Intelligent Systems

Many systems today look intelligent. They generate fluent text, classify images, detect patterns, and produce predictions with impressive accuracy. When seen in isolation, these outputs can feel like a breakthrough. Teams watch a demonstration, see something that appears human-like, and assume value has been created. This is where the illusion begins.

Intelligence, in practice, is not about how convincing an output looks. It is about whether something changes as a result of that output. A system can appear remarkably smart and still be irrelevant to the work it was meant to support. The gap between appearance and impact is one of the most common reasons AI initiatives disappoint.

In many organizations, intelligence is confused with insight. A system produces a prediction, a score, or a recommendation, and that result is treated as an achievement on its own. Dashboards look sophisticated. Reports grow more complex. Yet nothing downstream actually changes. Decisions remain the same. Processes remain the same. People continue to work around the system rather than with it.

This happens because outputs are easy to admire, while impact is harder to measure. It is simple to demonstrate that a system can generate something impressive. It is far more difficult to show that the output leads to better choices, faster action, or reduced risk. As a result, teams optimize for what can be shown rather than for what truly matters.

Another reason the illusion persists is that intelligent-looking systems often operate at a distance from real work. They exist as separate tools, reports, or experiments. They are not embedded into the moments where decisions are made. When intelligence arrives too late, or without context, it becomes background noise. People glance at it, acknowledge it, and then fall back on habits and experience.

There is also a psychological component. When a system looks sophisticated, people assume it must be useful. Questioning its value feels uncomfortable, especially after time and money have been invested. This creates a quiet pressure to accept outputs as meaningful, even when no one can clearly explain how they are being used.

Over time, this leads to a familiar pattern. Systems continue to improve technically while their practical relevance stays flat. Accuracy increases. Models become more refined. Yet the organization does not feel different. The work does not feel easier. Decisions do not feel clearer. The intelligence exists, but it floats above the reality of daily operations.

The core problem is not a lack of capability. It is a mismatch between intelligence and purpose. Intelligence without a clear role becomes decoration. It looks impressive, but it does not earn its place. Real value only appears when intelligence is tightly connected to a specific decision, at a specific moment, for a specific outcome.

Recognizing this illusion is an important first step. It shifts attention away from how advanced a system appears and toward what it actually changes. When teams stop asking whether a system is intelligent and start asking whether it makes work meaningfully better, the conversation changes. That shift in thinking lays the foundation for everything that follows.

Decisions Are the Unit of Value

Organizations do not run on information. They run on decisions. Budgets are approved or rejected. Prices are adjusted or left unchanged. Customers are contacted, delayed, or ignored. Inventory is reordered or allowed to run low. These moments—often small and routine—are where work actually happens. Everything else exists to support them.

This is why decisions, not predictions or insights, are the true unit of value. Information only matters when it influences a choice. A system can generate accurate forecasts, detailed reports, or elegant analyses, but if no decision changes as a result, nothing of value has been created. The organization may feel more informed, but it does not behave differently.

In a business context, a decision is a commitment to act. It answers a practical question: What will we do now? That decision may be made by a person, supported by a system, or partially automated, but it always carries consequences. Time, money, and responsibility are attached to it. This is what separates decisions from insights. Insights explain. Decisions commit.

Many AI initiatives stop at insight. A model predicts customer churn. A system estimates demand. A score ranks risks. These outputs are often impressive, and they are often correct. Yet the organization still struggles to answer the next question: So what?

Who acts on this information? When? And how does it change what they would have done otherwise?

Consider a simple example. A sales team receives a weekly report identifying customers who are likely to leave. The report is accurate and well-designed. But the team is already overloaded. No one owns the follow-up. The report is read, acknowledged, and then forgotten. The prediction exists, but the decision does not. The value remains unrealized.

Now contrast this with a decision-centered approach. The same prediction is tied to a clear action: when a customer crosses a certain risk threshold, a retention offer is triggered or a call is scheduled. Ownership is defined. Timing is clear. The prediction no longer lives on a dashboard; it lives inside a decision process. Value appears not because the prediction improved, but because behavior changed.

This distinction explains why many organizations feel surrounded by intelligence yet unchanged by it. They invest heavily in systems that explain the world but hesitate to let those systems influence action. Often this hesitation is framed as caution, but more commonly it is a lack of decision clarity. No one has agreed on which decisions matter most, or how much autonomy a system should have in influencing them.

When AI is evaluated through the lens of decisions, priorities shift. Accuracy becomes a means, not a goal. Timeliness matters more than precision. Trust and accountability become design concerns, not afterthoughts. The question is no longer "How good is this model?" but "Which decision does this support, and what changes because of it?"

This way of thinking simplifies conversations. It cuts through complexity. Instead of debating tools or techniques, teams are forced to name the decisions that define their work. AI earns its place only when it helps those decisions become better, faster, or more consistent. Anything else may be interesting, but it is not yet valuable.

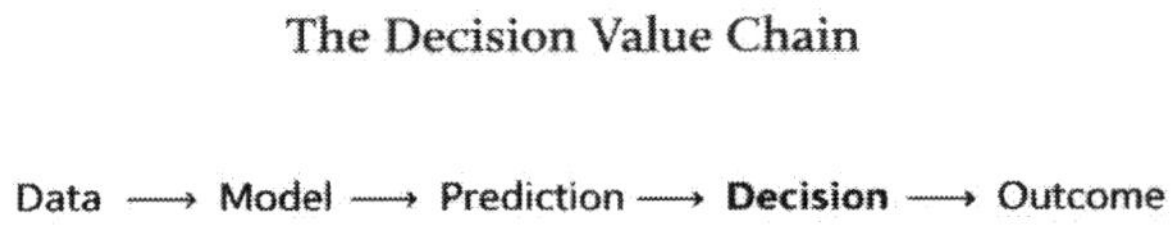

Figure 1. The Decision Value Chain

Value is created when decisions change.

Why Better Models Rarely Change Behavior

It is natural to assume that better technology leads to better outcomes. If a system becomes more accurate, more reliable, or more sophisticated, it should change how people work. In practice, this rarely happens. Many organizations improve their models steadily while day-to-day behavior remains almost exactly the same.

One reason is that human behavior does not respond linearly to technical improvement. Small gains in performance are often invisible to the people expected to act on them. From their perspective, the system still feels uncertain. If a recommendation was questionable before, it often remains questionable after an incremental improvement. Without a clear shift in confidence, behavior stays unchanged.

Trust plays a central role here. People do not change how they work simply because a system is better on paper. They change when they feel safe relying on it. That sense of safety comes from consistency, transparency, and experience over time—not from claims of improvement. If users cannot explain why a system suggests something, or if they have seen it fail in meaningful ways, improvements behind the scenes do little to restore confidence.

There is also hesitation rooted in responsibility. Acting on a system's output often feels like taking a personal risk. If the outcome is good, the credit is diffuse. If the outcome is bad, the blame is often personal. In such environments, sticking with familiar judgment feels safer than trusting an improved model. This dynamic quietly discourages adoption, even when systems perform well.

Organizational inertia amplifies these effects. Workflows are built around existing habits, approvals, and checks. Introducing new behavior requires more than better predictions; it requires changes to roles, incentives, and expectations. Without those changes, improved models are absorbed into old processes without altering them. The organization becomes technically more advanced but behaviorally unchanged.

Another overlooked factor is timing. Many systems deliver information at moments when decisions have effectively already been made. By the time a recommendation appears, people are committed to a course of action. Improving the quality of the recommendation does not change that reality. Behavior only shifts when intelligence arrives early enough to influence choice, not after momentum has taken over.

This is why teams are often surprised by the limited impact of technical progress. They focus on making systems smarter, assuming behavior will follow. Instead, they encounter resistance, indifference, or quiet avoidance. The issue is not that people reject intelligence; it is that intelligence alone does not address the conditions under which people are willing to change.

Real behavioral change requires more than better models. It requires clarity about which decisions matter, confidence in when and how a system should be used, and alignment with how people are evaluated and rewarded. When these elements are missing, improvements remain trapped inside the system.

Understanding this gap is essential. It shifts attention away from endless optimization and toward the human and organizational factors that actually determine impact. Until those factors are addressed, better models will continue to exist alongside unchanged behavior, impressive in theory and limited in practice.

The Decision Gap

Between what a system produces and what an organization actually does lies a quiet but powerful gap. AI systems generate outputs—scores, alerts, recommendations—but decisions happen elsewhere, often later, and under different conditions. This distance is where much of AI's potential disappears.

The decision gap forms when outputs are treated as information rather than as part of a decision process. A system may flag a risk, suggest an opportunity, or highlight an anomaly, but no clear path exists from that signal to action. The output arrives, is noticed, and then waits. Without a defined next step, it slowly loses relevance.

One common cause of this gap is the handoff between systems and people. Intelligence is produced in one place and consumed in another. A report is sent to a team. A dashboard is reviewed in a meeting. An alert appears in a shared inbox. Each handoff introduces delay, interpretation, and uncertainty. By the time responsibility reaches a person who could act, the context may be incomplete or the moment may have passed.

I once saw this clearly in a mid-sized financial services firm introducing AI to assist credit approval decisions. The model generated a risk score for every application. Technically, it performed well. The outputs were consistent and statistically sound. But the score was displayed in a separate dashboard that loan officers checked at the end of the day. By then, many decisions had already been made based on habit and workload pressure. The intelligence existed. The decision process did not change. The gap absorbed the value.

Unclear ownership makes this worse. When it is not obvious who is responsible for acting on an output, everyone assumes someone else will handle it. The system does its job, but the organization does not. Over time, people learn that paying attention to these outputs is optional. The system becomes background noise rather than a driver of action.

The gap is also reinforced by organizational boundaries. Outputs often cross teams, departments, or levels of seniority. A system may surface an issue, but resolving it requires coordination, approval, or resources that sit elsewhere. If acting on the information creates friction or extra work, it is quietly deprioritized. The intelligence remains accurate, but its influence fades.

Another source of the decision gap is timing. Outputs are frequently delivered on fixed schedules or through static channels, while decisions are made dynamically. When intelligence does not align with the rhythm of work, it feels disconnected. People may acknowledge it, but they do not incorporate it into their flow. The system speaks, but it speaks at the wrong moment.

Importantly, the decision gap is rarely intentional. Teams do not design systems to be ignored. It emerges gradually as outputs are added without redesigning how decisions are made. Each new system promises insight, but few address the full journey from signal to action. The result is an accumulation of intelligence with diminishing influence.

Closing this gap requires a shift in focus. Instead of asking what a system can produce, organizations must ask where a decision begins and ends. Who notices the signal? Who has the authority to act? What happens next? When these questions remain unanswered, even the most sophisticated systems struggle to matter.

Recognizing the decision gap is an important step toward practical AI. It reframes the problem from one of capability to one of connection. The challenge is not generating better outputs, but ensuring those outputs arrive in a place where action is possible and responsibility is clear. Only then can intelligence move from observation to impact.

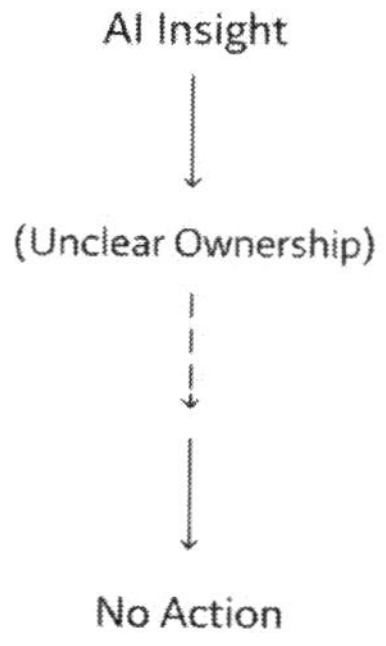

Figure 2. The Decision Gap

Who Owns the Decision?

Every decision has an owner, even when no one is explicitly named. In many AI systems, that ownership is vague, shared, or quietly avoided. This ambiguity is one of the most reliable ways to undermine impact. When it is unclear who is responsible for acting on an output, the system's influence fades, regardless of how accurate or timely it is.

Unclear ownership often emerges unintentionally. Teams focus on building systems that generate intelligence and assume responsibility will sort itself out later. In practice, later rarely comes. Outputs are delivered to groups rather than individuals, or to roles without the authority to act. The system speaks, but no one is clearly expected to respond.

Accountability complicates this further. Decisions carry risk, and risk carries blame. When outcomes are uncertain, people become cautious about attaching their name to an action influenced by a system. If a decision turns out well, credit is often shared. If it turns out poorly, responsibility can become very personal. In such environments, deferring to human judgment feels safer than relying on an automated or assisted recommendation.

This dynamic creates a subtle resistance. People may consult the system, but they hesitate to let it influence their final choice. The output becomes advisory in the weakest sense—something to glance at rather than something to act on. Over time, this behavior becomes normalized. The system exists, but its role is peripheral.

Leadership dynamics play a significant role here. When leaders send mixed signals about responsibility, uncertainty spreads. If leadership expects teams to use AI but also penalizes mistakes harshly, the safest response is avoidance. Ownership cannot exist without psychological safety. People must know not only what they are responsible for, but also how outcomes will be judged.

Treating decision ownership as a design problem changes the conversation. Instead of asking who should be blamed when something goes wrong, teams ask how responsibility should be distributed in the system itself. Which decisions should remain human-led? Which can be partially automated? Where is oversight required, and where is autonomy appropriate? These are design choices, not cultural slogans.

Clear ownership does not mean rigid control. It means clarity. Someone knows when a decision is theirs to make, what inputs they are expected to consider, and how much discretion they have. When this clarity exists, systems gain relevance. Outputs are no longer suggestions floating in space; they become inputs to a defined responsibility.

Without this clarity, AI systems struggle to earn trust. People may admire them, reference them, or cite them in meetings, but they will not rely on them. Ownership turns intelligence into action. When it is missing, even the most capable systems remain underused, not because they are flawed, but because no one truly owns the decisions they are meant to support.

From Information to Intervention

Most AI systems begin their life as sources of information. They observe patterns, highlight risks, or suggest possibilities. In this role, they behave much like reports or dashboards: they inform, but they do not act. This is a comfortable starting point. Informational systems feel safe because they leave control firmly in human hands.

Intervention changes that balance. An intervening system does not merely describe what is happening; it influences what happens next. It may prioritize cases, trigger actions, or block certain choices. The moment a system intervenes, it becomes part of the decision itself rather than a passive observer. This shift is where both value and tension increase.

The distinction between information and intervention is not about technology. It is about responsibility. Informational systems distribute responsibility broadly. Many people may see the output, but no one is forced to act. Intervening systems concentrate responsibility. Someone must decide where and how the system is allowed to influence outcomes, and what happens when it is wrong.

Automation often enters the conversation here, but it is frequently framed in terms of efficiency. That framing is incomplete. The real question is not how much work can be automated, but how much risk an organization is willing to accept. Every automated intervention encodes a judgment about acceptable error, acceptable delay, and acceptable consequences. These judgments are rarely neutral.

Human oversight plays a critical role in managing this risk. In some decisions, speed and consistency matter more than nuance. In others, context and discretion are essential. Knowing the difference is a design challenge, not a technical one. Systems that intervene too aggressively can erode trust. Systems that never intervene fail to deliver value.

There is also a tendency to treat intervention as a binary choice: either a system acts automatically or it does not. In reality, there is a spectrum. Systems can nudge rather than decide, constrain options rather than select them, or escalate decisions rather than resolve them. These intermediate forms often provide the best balance between control and impact.

Organizations struggle with this transition because it forces explicit choices. It is easier to build systems that inform and leave responsibility vague. Moving toward intervention requires naming who is accountable, what thresholds matter, and how exceptions are handled. These conversations can be uncomfortable, but avoiding them limits the system's relevance.

The most effective AI systems are intentional about where they sit on this spectrum. They intervene where the cost of delay or inconsistency is high, and they defer to humans where judgment and context matter most. They are designed with an understanding that intervention is not just a technical capability, but an organizational commitment.

Progress from information to intervention is not about replacing people. It is about deciding, deliberately, where systems should shape action and where humans should remain in control. When this balance is handled thoughtfully, AI becomes part of real work rather than an observer of it.

Designing AI Around Decisions

When teams begin with tools, design tends to follow capability. What can this system predict? What data is available? What models perform best? These questions feel concrete and productive, but they often lead systems away from real impact. Design becomes an exercise in assembling components rather than shaping outcomes.

Starting with decisions changes this trajectory. Instead of asking what a system can do, teams ask what choice needs to be made differently. The focus shifts from possibility to purpose. Design becomes an act of clarification rather than accumulation.

A decision-first approach begins by naming the decision clearly. Not in abstract terms, but in operational language. Who is deciding? What options exist? What constraints matter? What happens if the decision is delayed or wrong? These questions narrow the problem space quickly. They remove ambiguity before any technical work begins.

Once a decision is clear, constraints naturally surface. Some decisions tolerate uncertainty; others do not. Some require speed; others require explanation. Some can be automated safely; others demand human judgment. These constraints are not limitations to work around. They are design inputs. They shape what kind of intelligence is useful and what kind is irrelevant.

Outcomes also become easier to define. Instead of measuring success by system performance, teams can evaluate whether decisions improve. Are choices made earlier? Are they more consistent? Are fewer cases escalated unnecessarily? These outcomes are closer to real work and easier for organizations to recognize as value.

This approach stands in contrast to tool-first design. Tool-first projects often begin with excitement about new capabilities. Teams explore what is possible, build prototypes, and refine models. Only later do they ask how the system fits into decision-making. By that point, the design is already constrained by earlier choices. The system may be impressive, but misaligned.

Decision-first design reverses this order. Tools are selected only after the decision context is understood. Data is gathered because it informs a specific choice, not because it is available. Complexity is added reluctantly, not enthusiastically. The system grows around the decision rather than forcing the decision to adapt to the system.

This shift also simplifies communication. Stakeholders can discuss decisions more easily than technology. They may disagree, but the conversation stays grounded in work rather than abstraction. This shared understanding reduces friction and helps align expectations early.

Designing around decisions does not reduce technical ambition; it channels it. It ensures that effort is spent where it matters most. Systems built this way tend to be smaller, clearer, and more resilient. They do fewer things, but they do them with purpose.

When decisions are treated as the center of design, AI stops being a collection of features and starts becoming part of how work is actually done.

Why This Changes Everything

When decisions become the starting point, many familiar problems begin to dissolve quietly. Systems become simpler, not because ambition is lowered, but because unnecessary complexity loses its justification. Work that once felt heavy becomes more focused. Effort shifts from building impressive capabilities to supporting meaningful action.

Decision-first thinking reduces waste by narrowing scope early. When teams agree on which decisions matter, they stop building systems that explain everything and start building systems that support something specific. This focus prevents over-collection of data, over-engineering of models, and over-investment in features that never influence behavior. Resources are spent where they can actually change outcomes.

Simplification follows naturally. Systems designed around decisions tend to have clearer boundaries. They know what they are responsible for and, just as importantly, what they are not. This clarity makes them easier to maintain, easier to trust, and easier to evolve. Instead of growing in all directions, they deepen where it counts.

The impact extends beyond technology. Decision-first thinking reshapes conversations inside organizations. Teams talk less about tools and more about responsibility. They discuss trade-offs openly rather than hiding them behind technical language. This transparency encourages maturity. People become more comfortable acknowledging uncertainty and more deliberate about how they manage it.

Culturally, this shift reduces friction between technical and non-technical roles. Decisions provide a shared language. Engineers, managers, and leaders can align around what needs to change without debating implementation details prematurely. This alignment builds trust and reduces the cycle of misinterpretation that often surrounds complex systems.

Over time, organizations that think this way develop a different relationship with AI. They stop chasing novelty and start valuing reliability. They accept that intelligence is not a spectacle but a quiet support. Success is measured not by how advanced a system appears, but by how seamlessly it fits into work.

This is what maturity looks like in practice. Not an accumulation of sophisticated systems, but a growing ability to decide well under uncertainty. AI becomes less visible as it becomes more useful. It fades into the background, where it belongs.

The change is subtle, but its effects are durable. When decisions come first, systems age better, teams learn faster, and progress feels steady rather than fragile. This shift does not promise transformation overnight. It offers something more sustainable: clarity, restraint, and long-term impact.

A Simple Test for Any AI Idea

When ideas about AI surface, they often arrive wrapped in excitement. A new capability appears promising, and the instinct is to explore it quickly before falling behind. In these moments, clarity matters more than speed. A simple test can help separate ideas worth pursuing from those likely to disappoint.

The first question is straightforward: What decision will this change? Not what insight it will produce, not what pattern it will reveal, but which specific choice will be made differently. If the answer is vague, the idea is not ready. Many initiatives stall because they begin with curiosity rather than commitment. Naming the decision forces that commitment early.

This question immediately exposes gaps. If no one can say who makes the decision, when it is made, or what alternatives exist, the system has nowhere to land. The idea may still be interesting, but it is not yet valuable. Clarifying the decision often leads to a smaller, sharper scope or reveals that AI is unnecessary.

The second question follows naturally: What happens if the system is wrong? Every decision carries risk, and AI changes how that risk is distributed. If a wrong recommendation leads to minor inconvenience, automation may be acceptable. If it leads to serious harm, delay, or reputational damage, stronger oversight is required. This question shifts attention from possibility to responsibility.

Applied together, these questions ground discussions that might otherwise drift into abstraction. Consider a proposal to predict customer behavior. Asking which decision will change may reveal that the organization has no agreed response to the prediction. Asking what happens if the system is wrong may uncover constraints that were not initially considered. In many cases, the idea becomes clearer. In others, it quietly loses momentum, saving time and resources.

Importantly, failing this test is not a failure. It is feedback. It signals that more thinking is needed before building anything. Some ideas pass easily because the decision is obvious and the risk is manageable. Others require refinement. A few should be abandoned altogether.

These questions are intentionally simple. They do not require technical expertise, and they do not depend on tools or trends. They can be asked in meetings, during planning, or at the start of a project. Their value lies in what they prevent: unclear goals, misplaced effort, and systems that impress but do not matter.

Used consistently, this test creates discipline. It encourages teams to slow down just enough to think clearly. Over time, it builds a shared understanding that AI is not about what can be built, but about what should be changed.

A Calm Reset

It is tempting to talk about AI in terms of capability. Faster models, better predictions, more automation. This language feels concrete and reassuring. It suggests progress is measurable and linear. Yet, in real work, progress rarely follows that path. What matters is not how advanced a system appears, but whether it changes how choices are made.

Throughout this chapter, the focus has been deliberately narrow. Not because AI is simple, but because clarity is rare. Decisions are where complexity becomes real. They are where uncertainty meets responsibility. When AI is framed around decisions, its role becomes easier to understand and harder to exaggerate. It is no longer a promise of intelligence, but a support for judgment.

This perspective also invites restraint. Not every problem needs automation. Not every insight needs to be acted upon. Treating decisions as the center of value encourages selectivity. It rewards systems that fit naturally into work and quietly improve it, rather than those that demand attention without earning it.

Perhaps most importantly, this way of thinking restores balance. It reminds us that AI does not replace decision-making; it reshapes it. Humans remain accountable, even when systems assist. Responsibility does not disappear simply because intelligence becomes more accessible. If anything, it becomes more visible.

As you move forward, keep this lens close. When evaluating ideas, designs, or claims about AI, return to the decision being affected. Ask whether it truly changes, and whether that change matters. This habit alone can filter out much of the noise.

The next chapter looks at why so many efforts fail even when this seems obvious. Not because teams lack skill, but because expectations, incentives, and assumptions quietly work against them. Understanding those forces is the next step toward making AI matter in practice.

Chapter 2
Why AI Initiatives Fail Early

Failure Starts Before Technology

When AI projects fail, the failure is often attributed to technical shortcomings. Models were not accurate enough. Data was insufficient. Systems did not scale. While these issues are visible, they are rarely the root cause. In many cases, failure is already underway long before any meaningful technical work begins.

The earliest stage of an AI initiative is shaped by how the problem is framed. If the effort begins with a vague ambition—use AI, be more intelligent, stay competitive—it lacks a clear anchor. These goals sound reasonable, but they do not define what should change in practice. Without that clarity, everything that follows drifts.

Mindset plays a quiet but decisive role. When AI is approached as a solution in search of a problem, teams are encouraged to explore possibilities rather than commit to outcomes. Exploration has value, but without direction it becomes an end in itself. Progress is measured by activity—meetings, prototypes, presentations—rather than by meaningful movement toward a specific goal.

Early assumptions also shape expectations in subtle ways. There is often an implicit belief that intelligence, once introduced, will naturally improve results. This assumption reduces the perceived need to make hard choices upfront. Decisions about scope, ownership, and trade-offs are postponed. The project remains flexible, but it also remains fragile.

Another common assumption is that clarity will emerge later. Teams expect that once data is explored or a prototype is built, the right use case will reveal itself. In practice, this rarely happens. Technical exploration produces options, not priorities. Without a clear sense of what matters most, promising directions compete rather than converge.

Importantly, none of this reflects a lack of competence or effort. Teams involved in these projects are often skilled and motivated. The issue lies in how the work is initiated. When early framing is loose, technical excellence cannot compensate. Systems are built on shifting ground.

There is also a tendency to avoid early constraint. Narrowing the problem too soon feels risky. It can appear limiting or premature. Yet constraint is what gives projects shape. Without it, efforts expand in multiple directions, consuming time and attention without delivering focus.

By the time technical work begins, many of these patterns are already set. Expectations are diffuse. Success is loosely defined. Responsibility is unclear. The project carries momentum, but not direction. At that point, even strong technical execution struggles to produce meaningful impact.

Recognizing that failure starts before technology reframes how AI work should begin. It emphasizes the importance of early thinking over early building. When projects invest in clarity at the start—about purpose, decisions, and outcomes—they reduce the risk that technology will be asked to solve problems it was never designed to address.

The Myth of the Technical Fix

When organizations struggle, technology often feels like a clean solution. It promises progress without confrontation. Better tools, smarter systems, and more advanced models suggest improvement without forcing difficult conversations. This belief is especially strong with AI, where technical capability is often mistaken for organizational change.

The myth of the technical fix rests on a simple assumption: if the system is good enough, the problem will resolve itself. Delays, inefficiencies, and poor decisions are attributed to a lack of intelligence. Add more intelligence, and behavior will improve. This framing is comforting because it keeps the problem external. The issue is not how the organization operates, but what it lacks.

In practice, this belief often masks deeper questions. Which decisions actually matter? Who is responsible for them? What trade-offs are acceptable? These questions are uncomfortable because they expose misalignment, unclear authority, or conflicting incentives. Turning to technology allows teams to postpone answering them.

Technical solutions also create the appearance of action. Building or acquiring a system feels productive. Progress can be demonstrated through milestones, prototypes, and metrics. Meanwhile, the underlying issues remain untouched. The organization moves, but not necessarily forward.

This pattern is not driven by bad intent. It emerges because technical work is easier to scope than organizational change. Systems can be specified, built, and measured. Cultural and structural issues are harder to define and slower to address. As a result, technology becomes a proxy for progress.

Over time, the myth reinforces itself. When early attempts fail, the response is often to invest further in technology rather than revisit assumptions. More data is gathered. Models are refined. Complexity increases. Each step deepens commitment while avoiding the original questions. The organization becomes technically richer but no closer to resolving the problem it set out to solve.

There is also a subtle transfer of responsibility. When outcomes disappoint, the system becomes the focus of critique. It was not accurate enough. It was not sophisticated enough. This framing protects existing structures from scrutiny. The possibility that the problem lies in how decisions are made or incentives are set remains unexamined.

Recognizing the myth of the technical fix does not mean rejecting technology. It means understanding its limits. Technology amplifies existing patterns; it does not replace them. If decision-making is unclear, AI will not clarify it. If incentives are misaligned, intelligence will not realign them.

Unclear Success Looks Like Progress

When success is not clearly defined, almost any activity can be interpreted as progress. This is especially true in AI projects, where complexity and novelty make it easy to mistake motion for movement. Teams build, test, present, and refine, and each step feels productive. Yet the organization may be no closer to achieving something that actually matters.

Vague goals create this illusion. Objectives like improve efficiency, use data better, or be more intelligent sound reasonable, but they lack boundaries. Without a concrete definition of success, it becomes difficult to say whether a project is working or merely continuing. Effort fills the space where clarity should be.

Demos are a common example. A system is shown producing impressive outputs. Stakeholders are reassured that progress is being made. The demonstration proves that something can be built, not that it should be used. Because no clear outcome was defined, the demo itself becomes the outcome. The project appears successful simply because it exists.

Metrics can reinforce this illusion. Teams track accuracy, coverage, or usage, assuming these indicators reflect value. While such measures can be useful, they are often disconnected from real-world impact. A system may be used frequently without changing decisions. It may perform well according to internal metrics while leaving the underlying problem untouched. Numbers provide comfort, even when they measure the wrong thing.

Activity without outcome is another symptom. Meetings are held. Reports are generated. Updates are shared. Each action signals engagement, but none guarantee progress. When asked what has changed as a result, answers become abstract. The project feels alive, yet its purpose remains vague.

Simple organizational examples make this pattern clear. Consider a team tasked with improving customer experience through AI. They build models, analyze feedback, and present insights. But no one defines what improvement means in practice. Are response times shorter? Are complaints reduced? Without these answers, the team can work diligently while the customer experience remains unchanged.

This dynamic persists because unclear success is rarely challenged. As long as visible work is happening, questioning its value feels uncomfortable. Stopping to redefine success can feel like slowing down. In reality, it is the only way to ensure progress is real.

Clarity changes everything. When success is defined in terms of specific outcomes, activity becomes purposeful. Demos are evaluated against real needs. Metrics are chosen to reflect change, not just performance. Work that does not contribute to the goal becomes easier to stop.

Recognizing that unclear success can look like progress is an important step. It encourages teams to pause, define what they are aiming for, and measure what actually matters. Without that clarity, projects may continue indefinitely, appearing successful while delivering little of lasting value.

Expectations vs Reality

AI projects often begin with high expectations. There is an implicit belief that intelligence will arrive quickly, operate reliably, and produce clear answers. These expectations are rarely stated explicitly, but they shape how success and failure are judged. When reality does not match this imagined standard, disappointment follows—even when systems perform reasonably well.

One common expectation is certainty. AI outputs are often treated as answers rather than inputs. Predictions are expected to be correct, recommendations to be confident, and results to feel definitive. In practice, AI deals in probabilities and trade-offs. Its outputs are inherently uncertain. When this uncertainty is not acknowledged upfront, normal variation is experienced as failure.

Speed is another source of tension. There is a widespread assumption that intelligence should accelerate decisions immediately. If a system does not deliver visible improvement quickly, patience wears thin. This overlooks the time required for organizations to adapt. Even when intelligence is available, processes, habits, and incentives take longer to change. The system may be ready before the organization is.

Perceived intelligence also plays a role. Systems that appear human-like or sophisticated raise expectations beyond what they can sustain. When outputs feel fluent or insightful, people assume deeper understanding than actually exists. This creates a fragile relationship. The first visible mistake can dramatically erode trust, not because the system performed poorly, but because it failed to live up to an inflated image.

Disappointment often emerges quietly. A system works, but not as dramatically as hoped. It supports some decisions, but not all. It requires adjustment, oversight, and iteration. None of this is surprising from a practical perspective, but it clashes with the narrative of effortless intelligence. As enthusiasm fades, the project is labeled underwhelming rather than reassessed realistically.

Importantly, this disappointment does not mean the system has no value. It means expectations were misaligned. Reasonable performance can feel inadequate when it is compared to an imagined ideal. This mismatch leads organizations to abandon systems prematurely or to seek replacement rather than improvement.

Managing expectations is therefore not a communication task added at the end. It is a design responsibility from the beginning. Teams must be clear about what a system can and cannot do, how uncertainty will appear, and what kind of improvement is realistic. Without this clarity, even useful systems struggle to earn lasting trust.

When expectations are grounded, reality becomes easier to work with. Imperfection is accepted as part of decision-making rather than as a flaw. Progress is measured in meaningful change rather than spectacle. AI projects that survive this alignment may not feel magical, but they become dependable. And in real work, dependability matters far more than surprise.

Incentives Shape Outcomes

How people are evaluated has a stronger influence on behavior than how systems are designed. This is true in general, and it is especially true in AI projects. Incentives quietly shape what teams prioritize, what risks they take, and what outcomes they consider acceptable. When these incentives are misaligned with real impact, even well-designed systems struggle to matter.

In many organizations, success is measured through activity rather than outcomes. Teams are rewarded for delivering projects on time, meeting technical milestones, or demonstrating progress through reports and presentations. These signals encourage movement, but not necessarily direction. An AI initiative can appear successful because it produces visible artifacts, even if it changes little in practice.

This dynamic influences adoption as well. If individuals are evaluated on avoiding mistakes rather than improving decisions, they will behave cautiously. Using a new system introduces uncertainty. Ignoring it feels safer. When the cost of failure is personal and the benefit of success is diffuse, the rational choice is often to minimize exposure rather than pursue impact.

Teams also adapt to survive within their environment. When incentives favor short-term results, systems are optimized for immediate visibility rather than long-term usefulness. Quick wins are emphasized. Deeper integration is postponed. Over time, this creates a pattern where AI remains peripheral—useful in demonstrations, limited in real work.

Evaluation structures can further complicate matters. If performance is judged independently across roles or departments, shared responsibility becomes difficult. A system may benefit the organization as a whole while increasing workload or risk for a specific team. Without aligned incentives, that team has little reason to embrace it. Resistance emerges not from opposition to AI, but from rational self-preservation.

This is why adoption often stalls even when systems are technically sound. The issue is not understanding or capability; it is alignment. People respond to what is measured. If metrics reward caution, intelligence will be used cautiously. If metrics reward activity, activity will flourish regardless of impact.

Changing this does not require elaborate frameworks. It begins with recognizing that incentives are part of system design. Decisions about evaluation, ownership, and reward shape how intelligence is received. When these elements support meaningful use, adoption becomes natural. When they conflict, even the best systems feel optional.

Understanding how incentives shape outcomes helps explain why some AI efforts quietly succeed while others fade. It shifts attention away from individual behavior and toward the structures that guide it. When incentives and impact move in the same direction, intelligence has room to influence real work rather than remain a well-intentioned accessory.

The Cost of Misalignment

AI initiatives rarely fail because one group makes a clear mistake. More often, they falter because different parts of the organization move in slightly different directions. Leadership, technical teams, and users each approach the work with their own priorities and assumptions. When these perspectives are not aligned, progress becomes fragile.

Leadership often frames AI in terms of strategy and potential. The focus is on transformation, competitiveness, and long-term advantage. These goals are important, but they are abstract.

Without translation into concrete decisions and workflows, they remain aspirational. Teams below may struggle to connect this vision to their daily work.

Technical teams, on the other hand, tend to focus on feasibility and execution. They look for clear requirements, stable inputs, and achievable scope. When goals are loosely defined, they compensate by building what they can measure and control. The result may be technically sound systems that do not address the underlying intent of the initiative.

Users experience AI differently. Their concerns are immediate and practical. How does this system affect my work? Does it add steps, remove steps, or change responsibility? If these questions are unanswered, uncertainty grows. Even useful systems can feel disruptive when they arrive without context or support.

Misalignment emerges when these perspectives operate in parallel rather than together. Leadership assumes progress because something is being built. Technical teams assume success because milestones are met. Users assume irrelevance because their needs were not addressed. Each group acts rationally within its own frame, yet the system as a whole struggles.

Communication gaps amplify the problem. Feedback flows unevenly. Signals from users may not reach decision-makers. Constraints faced by technical teams may not be visible to leadership. Over time, misunderstandings accumulate. Adjustments become harder as commitments solidify.

Conflicting priorities further strain alignment. Leadership may push for speed. Teams may prioritize stability. Users may seek predictability. When these priorities clash, compromises are made implicitly rather than deliberately. The system reflects these compromises, often in ways that satisfy no one fully.

The cost of misalignment is not always immediate failure. More often, it appears as slow erosion. Enthusiasm fades. Usage plateaus. Maintenance becomes a burden rather than an investment. The system exists, but its influence shrinks.

Addressing misalignment requires more than better coordination. It requires shared clarity about purpose and decisions. When leadership, builders, and users align around what needs to change and why, trade-offs become explicit. Expectations adjust. Responsibility becomes clearer.

When alignment is treated as a continuous effort rather than a one-time agreement, AI initiatives gain resilience. They can adapt without losing direction. Without this alignment, even well-intentioned efforts struggle to move from promise to practice.

When Proof of Concept Becomes a Trap

Proof-of-concept projects play a special role in AI work. Unlike traditional software, AI systems can appear successful long before they are useful. A model performs well on historical data. Outputs look plausible. Results feel intelligent. This makes AI POCs particularly convincing — and particularly misleading.

In an AI context, a POC often demonstrates that something can be predicted or generated. What it does not demonstrate is whether that prediction changes a real decision, earns trust, or survives contact with day-to-day operations. Accuracy under controlled conditions is mistaken for readiness, and learning behavior is mistaken for understanding.

This creates false confidence. Stakeholders see a system perform well in a narrow setting and assume it will behave similarly in real work. What remains hidden are the conditions that matter most: noisy inputs, incomplete context, shifting priorities, and human judgment. AI systems are sensitive to these factors, yet POCs are designed to exclude them.

Another trap is how intelligence is interpreted. When outputs look reasonable, people project more reliability onto the system than it deserves. A recommendation that sounds confident is treated as stable, even if it is fragile. When the system later behaves unpredictably in production, trust collapses. The disappointment is not caused by poor performance, but by expectations formed during the POC.

AI POCs also delay essential decisions. Questions about ownership, intervention, and acceptable error are postponed because the project is still "experimental." In traditional software, functionality is the main uncertainty. In AI, behavior is. Avoiding these conversations early means the system is never tested against the conditions that actually matter.

Learning systems add another layer of illusion. A POC may improve over time within a controlled dataset, creating the impression that the system will naturally get better in production. In reality, learning amplifies whatever environment it is placed in. If the surrounding process is unclear, the system learns instability, not intelligence.

This is why many AI POCs never make the transition to real value. They prove technical possibility without proving operational relevance. They optimize for demonstration rather than durability. The organization becomes confident in the idea, but unprepared for the consequences.

AI POCs are useful only when they answer a specific question quickly — and then end. Do we have the right signal? Is this decision even worth supporting? Once those questions are answered, continuing to experiment delays the harder work of integration, responsibility, and trust.

Recognizing this trap is a sign of maturity. It allows teams to treat AI experiments as tools for learning, not substitutes for commitment. In AI work, the goal of a POC is not to prove intelligence, but to decide whether real change is worth pursuing.

Failure as a Systemic Outcome

When AI initiatives fail, the search for a cause often begins with individuals. Someone made the wrong choice. A team lacked expertise. A decision was poorly executed. While these explanations are familiar, they rarely capture the full picture. Most failures are not the result of isolated mistakes, but of systems that make failure likely.

Structures shape behavior long before people act. If decision-making authority is separated from execution, intelligence may be generated in one place and ignored in another. If responsibility is distributed across roles without clear ownership, no single person feels accountable for outcomes. These structural conditions persist regardless of who occupies the roles. Even capable, motivated teams struggle when the system around them works against alignment.

Processes reinforce these structures. Many organizations move projects through stages that emphasize approval, delivery, and reporting rather than learning and adjustment. Feedback loops are slow. Signals arrive after decisions are already locked in. In such environments, intelligence struggles to influence action. AI may surface insights, but the process offers no clear way to respond meaningfully.

The surrounding environment also matters. Teams operate under pressure, with limited time and competing priorities. New systems are introduced into already crowded workflows. If engaging with an AI system adds friction without immediate relief, it is quietly deprioritized. This behavior is not resistance; it is a rational response to the environment.

Consider a common scenario. A system identifies opportunities to reduce risk or improve outcomes. Acting on those signals requires coordination across teams and approval from multiple stakeholders. Each step introduces delay. Eventually, the moment passes. No one explicitly decides to ignore the system. Inaction emerges naturally from the structure and process.

These patterns explain why similar failures repeat across organizations. Different people. Different tools. Same results. The cause is not a lack of intelligence or effort, but a lack of fit between systems and the context in which they operate. Intelligence is added, but the surrounding conditions remain unchanged.

Viewing failure as systemic changes how improvement is approached. Instead of replacing people or endlessly refining technology, attention shifts to the conditions that shape behavior. Where are decisions made? How quickly can they change? What happens when intelligence conflicts with existing incentives or timelines?

This perspective does not remove accountability. It places it where it can be effective. When structures, processes, and environments support the use of intelligence, people can succeed. When they do not, failure becomes predictable rather than surprising.

Recognizing failure as a systemic outcome encourages realism. It reminds us that adding intelligence without adjusting context rarely produces lasting change. Without addressing the system around the system, new initiatives are likely to repeat the same patterns, regardless of how promising they appear.

What Successful Teams Do Differently

Teams that succeed with AI tend to differ in subtle but important ways from those that struggle early. The difference is rarely technical. It shows up in how uncertainty is handled, how decisions are owned, and how systems are woven into everyday work.

Successful teams accept uncertainty as a normal condition rather than a flaw. They do not expect AI to provide certainty or perfect answers. Instead, they treat outputs as inputs to judgment. This mindset allows them to use imperfect intelligence productively, without waiting for unrealistic levels of confidence. Teams that struggle often delay action until the system feels "good enough," which in practice means they delay indefinitely.

Decision ownership is another defining trait. Teams that apply AI effectively are explicit about who is responsible for acting on system outputs. This ownership is not symbolic. Someone knows when a decision is theirs to make, what information they are expected to consider, and how much discretion they have. In contrast, teams that treat AI as a technical initiative often distribute outputs broadly, assuming value will emerge naturally. Without clear ownership, responsibility dissolves.

Integration into daily work is where many efforts succeed or fail. Successful teams design AI to fit into existing workflows or deliberately reshape those workflows to accommodate it. Intelligence arrives at the moment decisions are made, not as a separate activity. Struggling teams often introduce AI as an add-on: another dashboard to check, another report to read. Over time, these systems compete for attention rather than earning it.

There is also a difference in how learning is approached. Teams that succeed observe how systems behave in practice and adjust accordingly. They expect iteration, not finality. When outputs are ignored or misused, they ask why, rather than assuming the technology is at fault. This feedback loop strengthens both the system and the surrounding process.

Teams that treat AI as a purely technical effort often focus on building and refining models while assuming adoption will follow. They invest heavily in capability and lightly in context. When behavior does not change, they interpret this as resistance rather than as a signal of misalignment.

What successful teams do differently is not dramatic. They spend more time clarifying decisions, less time showcasing intelligence. They accept responsibility early and adjust continuously. Over time, these small choices compound. AI becomes part of how work is done, not because it is impressive, but because it is trusted, timely, and clearly owned.

Before You Build Anything

When AI initiatives disappoint, the instinct is often to look for technical remedies. More data. Better models. Faster systems. These responses feel logical, but they arrive too late. By the time technology is being adjusted, many of the conditions for failure are already in place.

What undermines AI efforts most often is not a lack of capability, but a lack of clarity. Unclear purpose, diffuse ownership, and unspoken assumptions quietly shape outcomes long before code is written. Once a system is built, these issues become harder to see and even harder to correct. Technology amplifies whatever thinking preceded it.

This is why the earliest phase of AI work deserves the most attention. Not as a formality, but as a discipline. Before building anything, organizations must confront questions that cannot be delegated to systems. What decision needs to change? Who will own it? What uncertainty is acceptable? These questions are uncomfortable precisely because they expose trade-offs and responsibility.

Avoiding them creates momentum without direction. Projects move forward, but their destination remains unclear. When results fall short, the gap is attributed to execution rather than to the absence of agreement at the start. Over time, this pattern erodes trust in AI rather than strengthening it.

Pausing before building does not slow progress. It protects it. It ensures that intelligence is introduced where it can matter, rather than where it merely looks impressive. This pause is not about caution for its own sake. It is about choosing deliberately what deserves to be changed.

The next chapter looks more closely at objectives and clarity, not as abstract concepts,but as practical anchors for AI work. Understanding how to define success before building anything is what turns intelligence into impact. Without that foundation, even the most advanced systems struggle to earn their place in real work.

Chapter 3
The Discipline of Clear Objectives

Objectives Shape Everything

Every AI initiative begins with an objective, whether it is stated clearly or not. That objective acts as a quiet force, shaping every decision that follows. When it is well defined, it creates focus. When it is vague, it introduces ambiguity that spreads through the system and amplifies complexity.

Unclear objectives make it difficult to draw boundaries. Without a shared understanding of what needs to change, scope expands easily. Teams include additional use cases, edge conditions, and exceptions in an effort to be comprehensive. Each addition feels reasonable in isolation, but together they create systems that are harder to build, harder to explain, and harder to maintain.

Ambiguity also affects how choices are made along the way. When priorities are not clear, decisions are deferred or made inconsistently. Teams may pursue parallel directions, unsure which one matters most. This leads to duplication of effort and frequent rework. Time is spent refining parts of the system that may never influence real outcomes.

Cost increases in subtle ways. It does not always appear as a large upfront expense. Instead, it accumulates through prolonged timelines, additional coordination, and repeated adjustments. Each clarification arrives late, after commitments have been made.

Correcting course becomes more expensive than choosing a direction early.

System behavior is shaped by this ambiguity as well. When objectives are loosely defined, systems are designed to handle many scenarios rather than a specific one. They become flexible but fragile. Their behavior may appear intelligent, yet it is often inconsistent because it is trying to serve competing goals. This inconsistency undermines trust and makes adoption harder.

Unclear objectives also complicate evaluation. Without a clear target, it is difficult to say whether a system is working. Progress is measured through activity rather than impact. Teams may celebrate milestones while quietly questioning whether the effort is justified. Over time, this uncertainty erodes confidence in the initiative.

None of this reflects poor execution. It reflects the power of early ambiguity. Objectives that are not clarified at the start shape decisions indirectly, through assumptions and compromises. By the time problems are visible, they are embedded in the structure of the system.

Clear objectives simplify. They narrow scope, guide trade-offs, and make costs visible earlier. They allow teams to say no with confidence. In AI work, where uncertainty is already high, clarity at the objective level is not a luxury. It is the foundation that determines whether intelligence becomes an asset or a burden.

Vague Goals Create Expensive Systems

When goals are loosely defined, systems tend to grow in size and complexity without a corresponding increase in value. This pattern is common in AI work, where uncertainty is already high and ambition is often broad. Vague goals invite overbuilding as a form of insurance. Teams add more capability not because it is needed, but because it feels safer than choosing a narrow path.

Unclear goals make it difficult to decide what to leave out. When no single outcome is prioritized, every potential use case feels important. Teams attempt to accommodate multiple scenarios at once, designing systems that can do many things reasonably well rather than one thing clearly. Each additional capability increases fragility. Interactions multiply. Assumptions conflict. The system becomes harder to reason about.

Cost rises through accumulation. More data must be handled. More exceptions must be managed. More coordination is required across roles and teams. None of these costs appear dramatic on their own. Together, they create a system that is expensive to build and even more expensive to sustain. Maintenance becomes a continuous effort rather than a predictable routine.

Teams often compensate for uncertainty by adding layers. If the goal is unclear, they introduce flexibility. If outcomes are uncertain, they add safeguards. If usage is unpredictable, they support multiple pathways. These responses are understandable, but they compound the problem. Complexity becomes a substitute for clarity.

Fragility is the hidden consequence. Overbuilt systems are sensitive to change. Small adjustments ripple through many components. Simple improvements require careful negotiation. As a result, teams become cautious. Iteration slows. The system hardens around its original ambiguity.

Vague goals also affect how success is judged. Without clear outcomes, cost is justified by potential rather than by results. Systems are defended because they might be useful someday. This mindset makes it difficult to question whether the investment is still appropriate. Over time, sunk effort replaces deliberate choice.

The alternative is not simplicity for its own sake. It is precision. Clear goals allow teams to design systems that are intentionally limited. They do less, but they do it reliably. Costs are easier to anticipate. Trade-offs are explicit. When change is needed, it can be introduced without unraveling the entire structure.

In AI work, where complexity arrives easily, vague goals are an expensive starting point. They encourage systems to grow in the absence of direction. Clear goals act as constraints, and constraints are what keep systems both affordable and resilient.

Optimization Without Direction

Most AI systems are built by people who care deeply about intelligence. They want models to be more accurate, predictions to be sharper, and systems to behave more reliably under more conditions. This instinct is understandable—and often necessary. But it also creates one of the most common traps in applied AI: optimizing the system while real-world impact stands still.

When objectives are unclear, teams tend to optimize what they can see. They focus on internal signals: how confident the model feels, how consistent its outputs appear, how well it adapts over time. The system becomes more competent by its own standards. Yet the decisions it informs don't improve, outcomes don't change, and users don't behave differently. Intelligence increases, but usefulness does not.

This happens because optimization needs direction. Without a clear definition of what "better" means in the real world, optimization drifts inward. The system learns to perform well inside its own feedback loops rather than in the messy environment it was meant to shape. It's like polishing an engine without checking whether the car is actually going anywhere.

One manifestation of this trap is accuracy obsession. Accuracy feels objective and comforting. It provides a sense of progress without requiring uncomfortable conversations about judgment, responsibility, or trade-offs. Teams chase small gains because they are measurable and defensible. But accuracy is only meaningful relative to a decision. If the decision remains the same—or if no one trusts or acts on the system—then higher accuracy is mostly decorative. The model may be right more often, but nothing downstream changes.

Another form is continuous tuning. Modern AI systems invite endless refinement. There is always another adjustment, another edge case, another opportunity to make behavior smoother or more robust. This creates motion, which can be mistaken for momentum. Teams stay busy, systems evolve, and technical sophistication increases. But without revisiting the original purpose, tuning becomes circular. The system is improved relative to its previous version, not relative to the problem it was meant to solve.

Learning systems intensify this effect. When a system adapts automatically, it can appear alive, responsive, even intelligent. But learning is not inherently valuable. A system can learn patterns that don't matter, optimize behaviors that no one notices, or reinforce assumptions that were never questioned. Learning gives the illusion of progress while quietly narrowing the system's relevance.

The core issue is not technical—it's conceptual. Optimization answers the question "How do we get better?" but not "Better for what?" When that second question is unresolved, teams default to internal definitions of success. These definitions are often inherited from research culture or engineering norms rather than from real-world needs. Over time, the system becomes excellent at satisfying its builders and invisible to its users.

This is why AI projects can feel successful on paper and disappointing in practice. The model works. The system is stable. The dashboards look healthy. Yet decisions remain unchanged, workflows stay inefficient, and outcomes are flat. The intelligence is real, but it's misaligned with impact.

Avoiding optimization without direction doesn't mean rejecting improvement. It means anchoring improvement to decisions, behaviors, and consequences outside the system. It requires resisting the comfort of internal progress and asking harder questions about relevance. Without that anchor, AI systems risk becoming increasingly intelligent mirrors—reflecting effort and ingenuity back to their creators, while the world they were meant to affect remains exactly the same.

When Everyone Agrees, But on Nothing

Many AI initiatives begin with apparent consensus. Meetings end with nods. Documents reflect agreement. Everyone seems aligned on the importance of the effort. Yet beneath this surface harmony lies a quieter problem: people are agreeing in words, not in meaning.

Superficial alignment often forms around broad statements. Phrases like improve decision-making, use AI strategically, or be more data-driven sound uncontroversial. Each group hears something different in them. Leadership may imagine strategic transformation. Technical teams may hear a mandate to build intelligent systems. Users may expect practical tools that make their work easier. All believe they are aligned, yet they are moving toward different outcomes.

This hidden divergence matters more in AI initiatives than in many other projects. AI systems amplify assumptions. They force vague intentions into concrete behavior. When objectives are not shared, the system reflects this confusion. It tries to serve multiple interpretations at once and ends up serving none particularly well.

Organizational examples make this pattern clear. Consider an AI initiative intended to "support better decisions." One team focuses on generating more information. Another expects automated recommendations. A third assumes human judgment will remain central. The system is built to accommodate all three perspectives. The result is a tool that produces insights, suggestions, and alerts—but no one is quite sure how it should be used.

Because disagreement is implicit rather than explicit, it is difficult to address. Each group assumes others share its understanding. When results disappoint, frustration emerges without a clear target. The technology is questioned. The team is blamed. Rarely does anyone return to the original alignment and ask whether it was real.

Superficial agreement also delays hard trade-offs. Decisions about scope, ownership, and acceptable risk are postponed in the name of harmony. This avoidance feels cooperative, but it increases long-term cost. AI systems built on unresolved differences require ongoing negotiation and adjustment. They become fragile, sensitive to shifts in interpretation.

The impact is subtle but persistent. Progress appears steady, yet confidence erodes. Stakeholders sense that the system does not quite match their expectations. Usage remains inconsistent. Trust develops unevenly, if at all.

Real alignment is quieter and more specific. It requires naming what will change and what will not. It accepts that agreement may be uncomfortable before it becomes productive. In AI work, this clarity is not optional. When everyone agrees on the words but not the meaning, intelligence becomes a mirror of organizational ambiguity rather than a driver of better decisions.

Objectives vs Requirements

In many AI initiatives, early conversations feel concrete and productive. Lists are created. Capabilities are defined. Expectations are documented. Yet despite this apparent clarity, projects often drift. A common reason is that requirements have replaced objectives.

Objectives describe why something matters. They define what should change in the real world if the system succeeds. Requirements describe what the system should do. They specify behaviors, outputs, or features. Both are necessary, but they are not interchangeable. Confusing them creates a subtle but powerful source of failure.

When teams start with requirements, they move quickly into solution space. They define what the system should produce, how often, and in what form. This feels efficient. However, without clear objectives, these requirements float without context. They describe activity, not impact. The system may meet every requirement and still fail to matter.

This problem is amplified in AI projects because intelligence can be applied in many ways. A system can generate predictions, scores, alerts, or suggestions. Choosing among these options requires a clear sense of what outcome is desired. Without that clarity, requirements accumulate. Teams attempt to cover multiple possibilities, hoping value will emerge from flexibility.

Outcomes, by contrast, force prioritization. An objective might be to reduce risk, improve consistency, or support faster decisions. These statements do not prescribe features. They set direction. Requirements can then be evaluated based on whether they serve that direction. Features that do not contribute become easier to question or remove.

Confusing objectives with requirements also affects how success is judged. If success is defined as meeting requirements, the project can be declared complete once the system behaves as specified. Whether decisions actually change becomes secondary. This creates a false sense of achievement. The system works, but the organization remains the same.

Organizational examples are common. A team defines an AI initiative by listing what the system should deliver: reports, dashboards, recommendations. No one explicitly states what decision should improve as a result. When usage is low, the response is to add more features rather than revisit purpose. Complexity increases, but outcomes remain unchanged.

Clear objectives act as a filter. They help teams decide which requirements are essential and which are optional. They also provide a basis for trade-offs when constraints appear. Without objectives, every requirement feels equally important, and nothing can be safely simplified.

In AI work, where possibilities are broad and uncertainty is high, objectives provide stability. They anchor requirements to real-world change. When teams reverse the order—starting with objectives and then defining requirements—they reduce waste, improve focus, and increase the likelihood that intelligence will translate into meaningful impact.

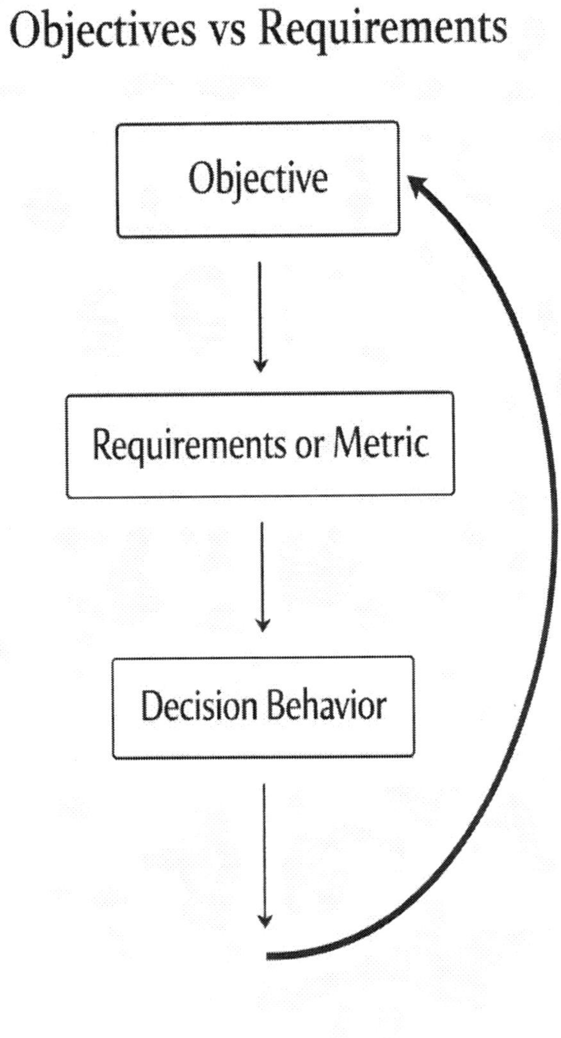

Figure 3. Objective–Metric–Behavior Alignment

The Cost You Don't See

When objectives are unclear, the most damaging costs rarely appear on budgets or timelines. They accumulate quietly, embedded in daily work, absorbed as normal friction. In AI initiatives, these hidden costs often outweigh the visible ones, precisely because they are harder to trace back to their source.

Rework is one of the earliest signs. Teams build systems based on an initial understanding that later turns out to be incomplete or misaligned. Adjustments are made. Features are revised. Scope shifts. None of this feels dramatic, but it consumes attention and energy. Over time, teams spend more effort correcting direction than moving forward. The work continues, yet progress slows.

Maintenance burden grows in a similar way. Systems built without clear objectives tend to support many scenarios rather than a specific outcome. They require ongoing attention to keep everything functioning acceptably. Small changes become risky because their impact is hard to predict. As a result, maintenance becomes cautious and time-consuming. What was meant to be intelligent support turns into a persistent obligation.

Trust erosion is a more subtle cost, but a more lasting one. When AI systems behave inconsistently or fail to deliver expected value, confidence declines. People stop relying on the system, not through explicit rejection, but through quiet avoidance. Once trust is lost, it is difficult to rebuild. Even improvements are viewed skeptically, filtered through past disappointment.

These costs are rarely attributed to objective clarity. Instead, they are explained away as growing pains or technical challenges. The organization adapts to them, treating friction as inevitable. Over time, this normalization makes it harder to question whether the system is worth sustaining in its current form.

Consider a common scenario. An AI system is introduced to "support better decisions." Because that objective is vague, usage varies widely. Some teams rely on it heavily. Others ignore it. The system must accommodate both patterns, increasing complexity. Maintenance grows. Trust fragments. No single failure occurs, yet the overall value diminishes.

Unclear objectives also drain morale. Teams sense when their work lacks direction. Effort feels less meaningful when outcomes are ambiguous. This erosion is gradual, but it affects how people engage with future initiatives. Skepticism replaces curiosity.

These hidden costs explain why some AI efforts feel expensive even when visible spending is modest. The real price is paid in attention, patience, and confidence. Clear objectives do not eliminate all costs, but they make them intentional. They reduce waste by aligning effort with purpose. In AI work, where uncertainty is unavoidable, clarity is what keeps that uncertainty from turning into an invisible tax on the organization.

Clarifying Objectives Is a Leadership Task

In AI initiatives, unclear objectives are often treated as a technical problem. Teams assume that once data is explored or systems are built, the right purpose will emerge. This belief places an unfair burden on technical teams and misunderstands the nature of AI work.

AI systems do not define intent. They operationalize it. When objectives are vague, intelligence amplifies ambiguity rather than resolving it. No amount of technical sophistication can compensate for missing direction about what decisions should change or what outcomes matter.

This is why objective clarity cannot be delegated downward. Technical teams are well equipped to assess feasibility, trade-offs, and constraints. They are not positioned to decide which organizational choices deserve to be influenced by AI. That responsibility sits with those who own outcomes, not implementations.

Leadership plays a distinct role here. Leaders determine which decisions are important enough to warrant intelligent support. They define acceptable uncertainty, risk tolerance, and accountability. These choices shape how AI behaves long before any system exists. When they are left implicit, systems are built to satisfy assumptions rather than intent.

In AI work, authority matters because uncertainty is unavoidable. Unlike deterministic systems, AI does not produce fixed answers. It produces signals that must be interpreted and acted upon. Deciding where that interpretation occurs, and who carries responsibility for action, is not a technical choice. It is an organizational one.

When leaders avoid this responsibility, objectives become compromises. Teams infer intent from incomplete signals. Systems are designed to satisfy multiple interpretations at once. The result is intelligence that looks capable but lacks direction. When outcomes disappoint, the technology is questioned rather than the framing that guided it.

Clear objective framing is not about control. It is about creating a stable reference point for decision-making. When leaders articulate what success looks like in decision terms, technical teams can design systems that support it. Boundaries become clearer. Trade-offs become explicit. Responsibility is shared rather than blurred.

In mature AI efforts, leadership does not dictate solutions. It provides clarity about purpose. This distinction is critical. Without it, AI initiatives inherit uncertainty from the top and reproduce it at scale. With it, intelligence has a chance to influence real work rather than reflect unresolved questions.

What Clear Objectives Enable

Clear objectives change how AI systems are experienced, not just how they are built. When purpose is well defined, many downstream challenges become easier to manage. Design choices simplify, risks become more visible, and adoption feels more natural rather than forced.

From a design perspective, clarity narrows focus. When teams know which decision an AI system is meant to support, they can design behavior around that moment. Unnecessary capabilities fall away. The system does less, but it does it more reliably. This restraint improves stability and makes the system easier to explain and maintain.

Risk is also easier to manage when objectives are explicit. AI systems always involve uncertainty, but not all uncertainty carries the same consequence. Clear objectives allow teams to distinguish between acceptable variation and unacceptable error. This makes it possible to put appropriate safeguards in place without overengineering. Risk becomes intentional rather than accidental.

Adoption improves because expectations are aligned. When people understand what an AI system is meant to do—and just as importantly, what it is not meant to do—they engage with it more confidently. The system arrives with a role, not a promise. This reduces hesitation and prevents disappointment caused by inflated assumptions.

Clear objectives also improve trust over time. Consistent behavior builds confidence, and consistency depends on knowing what the system is trying to achieve. When objectives are vague, behavior varies as interpretations shift. When objectives are clear, behavior stabilizes. Trust grows not because the system is impressive, but because it is predictable.

Downstream effects extend beyond the system itself. Clear objectives make feedback more meaningful. When outcomes are defined, it becomes easier to learn from use. Adjustments are guided by purpose rather than by guesswork. Teams can tell whether changes are moving the system closer to its goal.

Perhaps most importantly, clarity reduces friction. Conversations become more concrete. Decisions are easier to make. Trade-offs are easier to accept. In AI work, where complexity and uncertainty are unavoidable, clear objectives act as a stabilizing force.

They do not eliminate difficulty, but they ensure effort is directed. When objectives are clear, intelligence has a place to land. The system becomes a support for real work rather than another source of ambiguity.

A Practical Way to Test Objective Clarity

Objective clarity often feels subjective. Teams believe they are aligned until problems appear. In AI work, waiting for problems is expensive. Fortunately, clarity can be tested early with a small number of simple questions. These questions do not require technical knowledge. They reveal whether purpose is truly shared or only assumed.

The first question is: Which decision is supposed to change because of this AI system?
If the answer cannot be stated plainly, the objective is not clear.

Phrases like provide insights, support users, or improve outcomes indicate direction, not intent. A clear objective names a specific choice that someone will make differently. This question forces teams to move from aspiration to action.

When this question is applied, ambiguity surfaces quickly. Different stakeholders often describe different decisions. Each description may sound reasonable, but they cannot all be correct. This disagreement is valuable. It exposes assumptions while there is still time to resolve them. In AI initiatives, surfacing this early prevents systems from being built to satisfy multiple, conflicting purposes.

The second question is: Who will act on the system's output, and what happens if they do not?
This question tests ownership. If no one can answer confidently, the objective lacks accountability. AI systems cannot create responsibility. They can only support it. When ownership is unclear, outputs become optional. Adoption suffers not because the system fails, but because its role was never defined.

Together, these questions reveal whether an objective is operational or abstract. They shift the conversation from what the system might do to how work will actually change. They also expose hidden risks. If acting on the system has consequences that no one wants to own, that hesitation signals unresolved concern about the objective itself.

Using these questions early does not slow progress. It accelerates it by reducing rework. Teams spend less time debating features and more time aligning on purpose. When clarity exists, technical decisions become easier and more consistent.

In AI work, ambiguity scales quickly. A small lack of clarity at the start becomes a large source of friction later. These questions act as a simple checkpoint. If they can be answered clearly and consistently, the objective is likely sound. If not, the best next step is not to build, but to clarify.

Clarity Is the Cheapest Optimization

In AI work, optimization often arrives too early and clarity too late. Teams invest time refining systems, improving behavior, and reducing imperfections, while the underlying purpose remains loosely defined. This imbalance is costly. It directs effort toward making things better before deciding whether they matter.

Clarity is different. It does not require new tools or additional resources. It requires agreement. When objectives are clear, many forms of complexity disappear on their own. Systems become simpler because they are built for a specific decision. Risk becomes easier to manage because uncertainty is understood rather than assumed. Cost is reduced not by efficiency, but by restraint.

Technical optimization has limits. It improves what already exists. Clarity determines what should exist in the first place. In AI initiatives, this distinction is critical. Intelligence amplifies intent. When intent is unclear, optimization magnifies confusion. When intent is clear, even modest systems can have meaningful impact.

Clear objectives also protect organizations from chasing diminishing returns. Without clarity, improvement becomes endless. There is always something to adjust, refine, or enhance. With clarity, teams know when "good enough" is sufficient. This discipline preserves attention and focus.

Perhaps most importantly, clarity reduces disappointment. When expectations are grounded in purpose rather than possibility, outcomes feel more reliable. Trust grows because systems behave consistently within known boundaries. AI stops being a source of surprise and becomes a support for judgment.

As this chapter closes, it is worth pausing on a simple idea: many AI failures are not technical in nature. They are the result of decisions that were never made. Clarity is what turns intelligence into something useful rather than impressive.

The next chapter shifts perspective. It explores moments when the most responsible choice is not to apply AI at all. Understanding when to stop is as important as knowing how to build.

Chapter 4
Knowing When Not to Use AI

AI Is Not Always the Right Answer

The current conversation around AI often assumes that intelligence should be added wherever possible. If a problem exists, the instinct is to ask how AI can help. This assumption is understandable, but it overlooks an important reality: adding intelligence is not always beneficial. In some situations, it introduces new risks without solving the original problem.

AI systems behave differently from traditional software. Their outputs are probabilistic rather than deterministic. This means they offer likelihoods, patterns, and suggestions rather than fixed answers. In contexts where consistency and predictability matter more than adaptability, this uncertainty can be a disadvantage. A simple, stable process may outperform an intelligent one when the cost of variation is high.

False confidence is another risk. AI outputs often appear authoritative, even when uncertainty is present. When systems produce fluent or confident results, people may overestimate their reliability. This misplaced trust can lead to decisions being taken with less scrutiny than they deserve. In such cases, intelligence does not improve judgment; it weakens it.

Misplaced automation is a related concern. Some decisions benefit from human deliberation, context, and accountability. Automating these decisions can remove necessary friction. AI systems excel at pattern recognition, but they do not understand consequences in the way humans do. When automation replaces reflection rather than supporting it, outcomes suffer.

There are also situations where the problem is not informational. If goals are unclear, incentives are misaligned, or responsibility is diffused, adding AI does not address the root issue. Intelligence amplifies existing structures. When those structures are weak, AI magnifies their weaknesses rather than correcting them.

Importantly, choosing not to use AI is not a failure of innovation. It is a sign of judgment. Mature use of AI involves restraint as well as capability. Knowing when intelligence adds value requires understanding both the problem and the decision environment in which it exists.

This perspective shifts the role of AI from a default solution to a considered option. It encourages organizations to ask not only what AI can do, but what it should do. In doing so, they protect themselves from unnecessary complexity and risk.

AI is powerful when applied thoughtfully. It is also costly when applied indiscriminately. Recognizing that AI is not always the right answer is the first step toward using it where it truly matters.

The Cost of Adding Intelligence

Adding intelligence to a system is often framed as an upgrade. More insight, better decisions, improved outcomes. What is discussed less often are the costs that come with that intelligence. These costs are not primarily technical or financial. They are operational, cognitive, and organizational—and they persist long after a system is introduced.

Uncertainty is the first cost. AI systems do not produce fixed answers. They produce outputs that vary based on context, data, and time. This variability requires people to interpret results rather than simply follow them. Interpretation takes effort. It also introduces hesitation. In environments where clarity and speed are valued, this added cognitive load can slow work rather than accelerate it.

Learning behavior introduces another cost. AI systems change over time. Their behavior shifts as conditions change and feedback accumulates. While this adaptability is often presented as a strength, it also demands ongoing attention. Systems must be observed, questioned, and recalibrated. This work does not end after deployment. It becomes part of daily operations, even if it is not formally recognized as such.

Trust management is a less visible but equally important cost. Trust in AI is not static. It must be built, maintained, and occasionally repaired. Small inconsistencies or unexplained behavior can undermine confidence quickly. Once trust is lost, people either disengage or overcompensate by double-checking everything, reducing the system's value. Managing this trust requires communication, clarity, and patience.

There is also a cost to decision ownership. When AI influences outcomes, questions arise about responsibility. Who is accountable when a recommendation is followed and the result is poor? Ambiguity here creates friction. People may hesitate to act, or they may defer responsibility to the system. Both responses reduce effectiveness.

These costs explain why adding intelligence sometimes feels heavier than expected. The system works, but it demands attention. It introduces new forms of work that were not present before. If these demands are not anticipated, they are experienced as frustration rather than investment.

None of this argues against using AI. It argues for realism. Intelligence is not free. It shifts where effort is required. Organizations that acknowledge these costs can plan for them. Those that ignore them are surprised when benefits fail to materialize.

Understanding the true cost of adding intelligence allows teams to decide when it is worth paying. In some cases, the answer is yes. In others, simpler solutions provide more value. The key is recognizing that intelligence always comes with responsibility, and that responsibility has a price.

When Simpler Systems Work Better

AI is often introduced with the promise of adaptability. It can learn from patterns, adjust to changing conditions, and handle complexity that fixed logic cannot. These strengths are real, but they are not universally beneficial. In many situations, simpler systems outperform AI precisely because they are limited.

Deterministic systems behave the same way every time given the same input. This predictability is often undervalued. When outcomes must be consistent, auditable, or easily explained, stability matters more than flexibility. In such contexts, variation is a risk rather than an advantage. AI's probabilistic behavior, while powerful, introduces uncertainty that may be unacceptable.

Earlier in my career, working in networking and server infrastructure environments, uptime was not a theoretical metric. It was operational survival. Routing rules, failover mechanisms, access controls—these were not areas where "adaptive intelligence" was helpful. They required absolute clarity. A packet either followed the defined path or it did not. When something failed, teams needed immediate traceability, not probabilistic reasoning. In those contexts, deterministic logic was not a limitation. It was the safeguard.

Consider decisions that are tightly regulated or carry clear accountability. When rules are well understood and exceptions are rare, a fixed approach provides clarity. People know what to expect. When something goes wrong, it is easier to trace why. AI, by contrast, can produce outcomes that are harder to anticipate or explain, even when they are statistically reasonable. This opacity can undermine confidence, especially in high-responsibility environments.

Simplicity also reduces cognitive load. Systems that behave consistently require less interpretation. Users do not need to evaluate confidence levels or second-guess outputs. They can focus on execution rather than judgment. In fast-moving or high-pressure settings, this reliability can be more valuable than nuanced intelligence.

Explainability is another factor. In many organizations, decisions must be justified to others—customers, regulators, or colleagues. Deterministic logic provides a clear narrative: this input led to this outcome because of this rule. AI systems often struggle to offer explanations that feel equally concrete. Even when explanations exist, they may not align with how people reason about responsibility.

There is also a maintenance consideration. Simpler systems change only when people decide to change them. Their behavior remains stable over time. AI systems, by contrast, can drift as conditions evolve. This adaptability requires ongoing monitoring and adjustment. When the environment is stable, this added complexity offers little benefit.

Choosing simplicity is not a rejection of AI. It is an acknowledgment of context. Some problems are already well understood. Some decisions benefit more from consistency than from optimization. In these cases, adding intelligence complicates what is already clear.

Mature use of AI includes knowing when not to use it. Simpler systems work better when predictability, transparency, and control are the primary goals. Recognizing these situations prevents unnecessary risk and preserves trust. Intelligence is valuable, but only when it serves the nature of the decision rather than reshaping it unnecessarily.

Decisions That Should Not Be Automated

AI is often introduced with the promise of efficiency. Decisions can be made faster, more consistently, and at greater scale. While these benefits are real, they do not apply equally to all decisions. Some choices carry risks and responsibilities that make automation inappropriate, regardless of how capable the system appears.

Decisions with irreversible consequences are a clear example. When an outcome cannot be easily corrected, the cost of error is high. AI systems operate under uncertainty. Even when performance is strong overall, individual mistakes are unavoidable. In situations where a single wrong decision can cause lasting harm, human judgment should remain central. Automation in these cases removes a necessary layer of reflection.

Accountability is another limiting factor. Some decisions require a clear owner who can explain not only what was decided, but why. AI systems can provide outputs, but they cannot assume responsibility. When accountability is essential—whether for legal, ethical, or organizational reasons—automating the decision creates ambiguity. People may defer to the system while still being held responsible for its consequences. This gap undermines trust and clarity.

Ethical considerations further constrain automation. Decisions that affect fairness, dignity, or personal treatment often require context that AI systems cannot fully grasp. These decisions involve values, not just patterns. Automating them risks reducing complex human situations to simplified representations. Even when outcomes are statistically reasonable, they may feel unjust or insensitive to those affected.

There are also decisions that shape long-term direction rather than immediate action. Strategic choices involve trade-offs that extend beyond available data. They reflect priorities, risk appetite, and vision. AI can inform these discussions, but automating them assumes that past patterns can determine future intent. This assumption limits adaptability rather than enhancing it.

Importantly, these limits are not failures of AI. They are boundaries of its role. AI excels at identifying patterns and supporting judgment. It struggles when judgment itself is the core of the decision. Recognizing this distinction prevents misuse.

Automating inappropriate decisions often creates a false sense of progress. The system works, decisions are made quickly, and efficiency improves on the surface. Over time, however, the lack of human involvement becomes a liability. Trust erodes. Responsibility becomes unclear. Correcting mistakes becomes harder because the decision process has been abstracted away.

Mature AI use is not about maximizing automation. It is about choosing where intelligence supports human responsibility and where it should stop. Knowing which decisions should not be automated is a sign of restraint and judgment. In real work, this restraint protects both outcomes and the people affected by them.

When Data Is Not the Problem

Many AI initiatives begin with a familiar diagnosis: we need better data. Gaps in performance are attributed to missing information, incomplete records, or insufficient scale. Collecting more data feels like a practical response. It promises improvement without forcing difficult changes. Yet in many cases, data is not the real problem.

Organizations often struggle not because they lack information, but because they lack clarity about decisions. When it is unclear who decides what, or how information should be used, adding data does not resolve confusion. It increases it. AI systems thrive on patterns, but patterns only matter when they are tied to a clear purpose. Without that link, intelligence amplifies ambiguity rather than reducing it.

Process issues are frequently misread as data issues. If decisions are slow, inconsistent, or contested, the instinct is to assume that more insight will help. AI is introduced to analyze, predict, or recommend. The underlying process remains unchanged. Roles are still unclear. Responsibility is still diffused. The system produces outputs, but no one knows how to act on them.

AI makes this misdiagnosis more visible. Because AI can surface patterns quickly, it exposes the absence of agreement. Different stakeholders interpret outputs in different ways. Each interpretation seems reasonable, yet they lead to conflicting actions. The problem is not data quality; it is decision framing.

There is also a temptation to treat AI as a neutral arbiter. When disagreement exists, intelligence is expected to settle it. This expectation places too much weight on data and too little on judgment. AI does not resolve value conflicts. It reflects them. When objectives are unclear, outputs become a mirror of organizational ambiguity.

Over time, more data is added in response to dissatisfaction. Complexity increases. Maintenance grows. Trust erodes as systems become harder to understand and less predictable. The original issue—unclear decisions or weak processes—remains unaddressed.

Recognizing when data is not the problem requires restraint. It means pausing before collecting or analyzing more information and asking whether the organization is ready to use what it already has. In many cases, simplifying decisions or clarifying responsibility delivers more value than additional intelligence.

AI is powerful when applied to well-defined problems. When applied to poorly framed ones, it magnifies their weaknesses. Understanding this distinction protects organizations from unnecessary effort and disappointment. It ensures that intelligence is used to support clarity, not to compensate for its absence.

The Readiness Gap

Organizations often assess AI readiness by looking at technical capability. Do we have the data? Do we have the skills? Do we have the infrastructure? These questions are important, but they miss a more decisive factor. Whether AI should be used at all is usually determined by organizational readiness, not technical strength.

The readiness gap appears when an organization can build AI systems but cannot absorb them into real work. Intelligence is introduced, yet decisions remain unchanged. Outputs are produced, but ownership is unclear. The system exists, but its role is uncertain. This gap is not visible in technical evaluations. It emerges only when AI meets everyday operations.

I saw this clearly while working in a healthcare environment exploring AI-assisted diagnostics. Technically, the system performed well. It could identify patterns in imaging data with impressive consistency. But the real question was not accuracy. It was readiness. Who would rely on the output? Would a physician override it? Would it act as a second opinion? Or would it quietly sit in the background as a reference tool? The hospital had strong technical teams, but decision ownership was deeply human — and rightly so. Without clarity on how recommendations would be used in practice, the system remained an experiment rather than an operational tool.

Trust is a central element of readiness. AI systems influence decisions under uncertainty. For people to rely on them, they must believe the system behaves consistently and within understood limits. If trust is low, outputs are ignored or constantly questioned. In such environments, adding AI increases friction rather than reducing it. The system may be accurate, but it is not usable.

Decision ownership is equally critical. AI readiness requires clarity about who is responsible for acting on system outputs. When ownership is diffuse, intelligence becomes advisory by default. People assume someone else will decide. This hesitation is not resistance; it is a rational response to ambiguity. Without clear ownership, AI cannot move from information to action.

Process maturity shapes how intelligence is used. Organizations with stable decision processes can integrate AI more easily because roles and handoffs are already defined. In less mature environments, decisions are negotiated informally or revisited frequently. Introducing AI into these settings exposes fragility. The system highlights inconsistency rather than improving outcomes.

The readiness gap often explains why technically successful projects fail to deliver value. Teams focus on what they can build rather than on what the organization can sustain. Intelligence arrives before responsibility, and adaptation follows slowly, if at all.

Closing this gap does not require more technology. It requires aligning trust, ownership, and process. When these elements are in place, even modest AI systems can have meaningful impact. When they are absent, advanced systems struggle to matter.

Recognizing the readiness gap helps organizations choose timing wisely. Sometimes the right decision is to wait, clarify, and prepare. In AI work, readiness is not a prerequisite to check off. It is the condition that determines whether intelligence will support real decisions or simply reveal what is not yet ready to change.

Saying No as a Mature AI Decision

In many organizations, choosing not to use AI feels like a missed opportunity. Intelligence is available, tools are improving, and expectations are rising. Against this backdrop, saying no can appear cautious or outdated. In reality, it is often a sign of clarity and discipline.

AI introduces uncertainty by design. Its outputs are probabilistic, its behavior can shift over time, and its influence depends heavily on context. Deciding to use AI therefore means deciding to accept and manage that uncertainty. When an organization is not prepared to do so, restraint is not a failure. It is responsible judgment.

Mature teams understand that not every problem benefits from intelligence. Some decisions require consistency more than optimization. Others require accountability that cannot be shared with a system. In these cases, adding AI complicates rather than improves outcomes. Saying no protects clarity and trust.

There is also responsibility to consider. AI systems influence decisions, but they do not own consequences. When the impact of a decision is significant, someone must be willing to stand behind it. If no clear owner exists, introducing AI creates ambiguity. Choosing not to automate or augment such decisions preserves accountability rather than diluting it.

Saying no also reflects confidence in understanding the problem. It signals that the organization is not using AI to compensate for unclear objectives or weak processes. Instead of adding intelligence to create the appearance of progress, mature teams address foundational issues first. This sequencing prevents disappointment later.

Importantly, restraint does not close doors. It keeps options open. When conditions change—when objectives are clearer, processes are more stable, or trust is stronger—AI can be introduced thoughtfully. Saying no now does not mean never. It means not yet, and for good reason.

This perspective contrasts sharply with environments where AI is applied everywhere by default. In those settings, intelligence becomes background noise. Systems are built, but few are trusted. Adoption is uneven. Over time, skepticism grows. What began as ambition turns into fatigue.

Mature AI decisions balance capability with responsibility. They recognize that intelligence has a cost and that not every context is ready to pay it. Choosing not to use AI can be a deliberate act of focus. It reflects an understanding of both the power and the limits of intelligence.

In real work, discipline matters as much as innovation. Saying no when AI does not fit preserves credibility and creates space for intelligence to be used where it truly adds value.

What Happens When AI Is Forced

When AI is applied without clear fit, failure rarely arrives suddenly. It unfolds through small, predictable patterns. Systems are introduced with good intentions, yet they struggle to improve outcomes because the problem they were meant to solve was never suitable for intelligence in the first place.

One common pattern is model misuse. When AI outputs are not well aligned with decisions, people use them in unintended ways. Scores become rankings. Probabilities are treated as certainties. Suggestions are followed mechanically or ignored entirely. The system is not wrong; it is being asked to play a role it was never designed for.

Loss of trust follows quickly. Early inconsistencies or misunderstandings create doubt. Because the system was forced into a context where its limitations matter, mistakes feel more serious than they are. Confidence collapses not because AI is unreliable, but because expectations were unrealistic. Once trust is damaged, recovery is slow.

Operational friction is another outcome. AI systems introduced into unsuitable workflows add steps without removing any. People must interpret outputs, resolve ambiguity, and manage exceptions. Instead of simplifying work, intelligence increases cognitive load. Over time, users develop workarounds to avoid the system, undermining its purpose.

Forced AI also exposes gaps in responsibility. When outputs lead to poor outcomes, accountability becomes unclear. People may blame the system or distance themselves from decisions influenced by it. This ambiguity discourages use and erodes confidence further. The organization becomes hesitant to rely on intelligence at all.

These patterns reinforce each other. Misuse leads to mistrust. Mistrust leads to avoidance. Avoidance reduces learning, making the system less useful. The cycle continues until the AI initiative is quietly sidelined or replaced.

Importantly, these failures are not the result of poor execution. They arise from misalignment between the nature of the problem and the nature of AI. Intelligence amplifies existing structure. When that structure is weak or inappropriate, AI magnifies its weaknesses.

Recognizing what happens when AI is forced helps organizations make better choices. It shifts focus from capability to suitability. Not every problem needs intelligence. Some need clarity, stability, or human judgment.

When AI is applied where it does not belong, it creates friction rather than value. Understanding this pattern allows teams to avoid unnecessary disappointment and preserve trust for situations where intelligence can truly support real work.

A Simple Test for When Not to Use AI

Deciding whether to use AI does not require a complex framework. In many cases, one or two well-chosen questions are enough to reveal whether intelligence will add value or introduce unnecessary risk. These questions are not technical. They focus on how decisions are made and how uncertainty is handled.

The first question is: If this AI system is wrong, who feels the impact immediately?
This question surfaces responsibility and consequence. AI systems operate under uncertainty, and errors are unavoidable. If no one can clearly name who bears the cost of a wrong output—or if the impact is diffuse and hard to correct—then AI may not be appropriate. Decisions with immediate, personal, or irreversible consequences require clear ownership. Without it, intelligence introduces risk without accountability.

This question also exposes whether AI is being used to distance people from responsibility. If the system's output is meant to justify a decision rather than support one, that is a warning sign. AI should not be a shield. When ownership is unclear, restraint is often the safer choice.

The second question is: Would a stable, simpler approach be acceptable here?
This tests whether adaptability is truly needed. AI is valuable when conditions change and patterns matter. If the environment is stable and rules are well understood, probabilistic behavior may add complexity without benefit. In such cases, intelligence does not improve outcomes; it complicates them.

Asking this question reframes the conversation. Instead of asking what AI can do, it asks what the problem requires. If consistency, transparency, or predictability are more important than optimization, simpler systems may serve better. Choosing AI in these contexts often reflects habit rather than judgment.

Together, these questions help teams pause before committing. They do not reject AI outright. They ensure it is used intentionally. If the answers reveal unclear ownership or unnecessary uncertainty, the most responsible choice may be to delay or decline.

Using AI well is not about applying intelligence everywhere. It is about applying it where its strengths align with the nature of the decision. These simple tests protect teams from forcing intelligence into places where it does not belong.

In real work, saying no early prevents larger problems later. When AI passes these tests, it has a chance to support decisions meaningfully. When it does not, restraint preserves clarity, trust, and focus.

Restraint Is a Strength

In a field defined by rapid progress, restraint can feel counterintuitive. The pressure to apply AI everywhere is subtle but persistent. Capability expands, expectations rise, and the absence of intelligence can be mistaken for inaction. Yet mature use of AI requires a different posture. It values judgment over novelty.

Restraint begins with understanding what AI introduces, not just what it promises. Intelligence brings uncertainty, ongoing responsibility, and the need for trust. These are not incidental side effects. They shape how systems are used and how decisions are made. Choosing not to apply AI when these costs outweigh the benefits is a form of discipline, not hesitation.

This discipline protects organizations from erosion. When AI is used indiscriminately, confidence weakens. Systems multiply, but few are trusted. Over time, intelligence becomes background noise. By contrast, restraint preserves credibility. When AI appears, it has a purpose. When it does not, its absence is intentional.

Restraint also creates space for clarity. It encourages teams to address foundational issues before adding intelligence. Clear objectives, stable processes, and defined ownership make AI more effective when it is eventually introduced. Without these elements, intelligence amplifies confusion rather than resolving it.

Importantly, restraint does not limit ambition. It sharpens it. By resisting the urge to apply AI everywhere, organizations can focus on the decisions where intelligence truly matters. These targeted applications build trust and demonstrate value, creating a stronger foundation for future work.

As this chapter closes, the message is simple: using AI well is not about maximizing adoption. It is about making deliberate choices. Knowing when to stop is as important as knowing when to proceed.

The next chapter turns toward design and structure. It explores how architecture and thinking shape AI systems once the decision to use intelligence has been made. Restraint sets the stage for thoughtful design, ensuring that what is built serves real work rather than momentum alone.

Chapter 5
From Proof of Concept to Production

Why AI POCs Feel Like Progress

AI proof-of-concept projects often generate enthusiasm disproportionate to their impact. Teams demonstrate working systems, models produce convincing outputs, and early results appear promising. This sense of progress is real, but it is frequently disconnected from changes in real work.

One reason AI POCs feel successful is that they make intelligence visible. Patterns appear where none were obvious before. Predictions emerge from historical data. Systems respond in ways that feel adaptive and responsive. These behaviors create the impression that something meaningful has been achieved, even if no decision has yet been influenced.

Learning behavior adds to this effect. When a system improves as more data is introduced, it reinforces the sense of forward motion. Each improvement signals potential. Performance curves move in the right direction. This progress is tangible and easy to measure. It feels like advancement, even when its relevance to real outcomes remains untested.

AI POCs also reduce uncertainty in a specific way. They answer the question, can this be built? For teams facing new technology, this is reassuring. The system works in isolation. It produces outputs reliably. This technical confidence is often mistaken for readiness to deploy, though many non-technical questions remain unanswered.

Impressive outputs play a psychological role. AI systems often generate results that appear insightful or intelligent. These outputs are easy to showcase and easy to celebrate. They create artifacts that can be shared with stakeholders. The narrative of progress becomes visual and concrete, while the harder work of integration and decision change remains abstract.

Another factor is that POCs operate in a protected environment. Expectations are lower. Consequences are limited. The system does not yet carry responsibility. This safety allows experimentation without commitment. While valuable for learning, it can also create comfort. Progress feels real because risk is absent.

The danger lies in conflating momentum with impact. AI POCs demonstrate possibility, not value. They show what intelligence could do, not what it does. When this distinction is overlooked, projects stall at the demonstration stage. Energy is spent refining performance rather than defining purpose.

Understanding why AI POCs feel like progress helps teams place them in context. POCs are useful when they answer specific questions quickly. They become problematic when they substitute for decisions. Recognizing this difference prevents momentum from turning into illusion and allows intelligence to move beyond demonstration into real work.

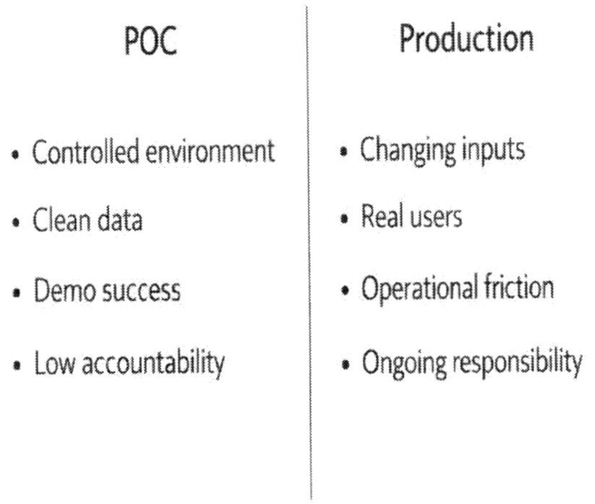

Figure 4. POC vs Production

Production Is Where AI Becomes Real

AI systems often perform impressively in controlled environments. During development or proof-of-concept stages, inputs are known, expectations are managed, and outcomes are observed without consequence. In these conditions, intelligence appears reliable. Production changes that reality. It is where AI stops being a demonstration and starts interacting with real work.

One reason AI systems struggle in production is uncertainty. Real environments are messy. Inputs change in subtle ways. Data arrives late, incomplete, or differently structured than expected. These variations may be insignificant to humans, but they can alter how AI systems behave. What looked stable in isolation becomes sensitive under real conditions.

Human interaction introduces another layer of complexity. In production, AI outputs are interpreted, questioned, and sometimes ignored. People use systems in ways that differ from original assumptions. Some rely on them heavily. Others use them selectively. This variability affects outcomes. AI systems do not operate alone; they operate within human judgment.

Production also exposes the cost of learning behavior. AI systems adapt over time, intentionally or unintentionally. Changes in context, feedback, or usage patterns influence performance. Without careful attention, behavior drifts. This drift is rarely visible immediately. It accumulates, creating discrepancies between expected and actual behavior.

In production, AI systems must also fit into existing processes. Decisions are made under time pressure, with competing priorities. Intelligence must arrive at the right moment and in the right form. If it does not, it is bypassed. A system can be accurate and still irrelevant if it does not align with how work is actually done.

Responsibility becomes unavoidable in production. When AI outputs influence outcomes, accountability matters. People want to know when to trust the system and when to override it. Ambiguity here leads to hesitation or over-reliance. Both reduce effectiveness.

These challenges explain why success in isolation does not guarantee success in production. Production reveals what was assumed, what was ignored, and what was misunderstood. It tests not just the system, but the organization's readiness to live with intelligence.

Understanding that production is where AI becomes real reframes success. It shifts focus from performance to integration, from potential to impact. AI creates value only when it survives contact with real work and continues to support decisions over time.

Accuracy Is Not the Same as Reliability

AI systems are often judged by how well they perform in controlled settings. When outputs appear correct and consistent during testing, confidence grows. Accuracy becomes the headline measure of success. Yet in real work, accuracy alone is rarely sufficient. What matters more is reliability over time.

Accuracy describes how often a system produces the expected result under known conditions. Reliability describes how a system behaves when conditions change, pressures increase, and human judgment enters the loop. An AI system can be accurate in isolation and still unreliable in practice.

One reason for this gap is variability. Real environments are not stable. Inputs shift subtly. Context changes. Usage patterns evolve. An accurate system may perform well most of the time but behave unpredictably at the edges. These moments matter disproportionately. They shape trust more than routine success.

Predictability is central to reliability. People need to understand how a system will behave, not just whether it is usually correct. If outputs fluctuate without clear reason, confidence erodes. Users begin to hesitate, double-check, or ignore the system entirely. Reliability is as much about expectation as performance.

Trust develops through repeated experience. It is built when a system behaves consistently within understood limits. Occasional errors are tolerated when behavior is predictable. Unexpected behavior, even when rare, undermines confidence. In AI systems, learning behavior can make this challenge harder. Changes intended to improve performance may alter how outputs are perceived.

Reliability also depends on alignment with real decisions. An accurate output delivered at the wrong time or in an unusable form fails to support work. Reliability includes availability, timing, and relevance. A system that is correct but inconvenient becomes unreliable in practice.

Another factor is human interpretation. AI outputs rarely act alone. They are read, questioned, and acted upon by people. Inconsistent interpretation can make a reliable system appear unreliable. This interaction highlights that reliability is a property of the system and its context, not the model alone.

Focusing only on accuracy encourages narrow optimization. Teams refine performance without considering how the system will be used day after day. Reliability requires a broader view. It asks whether the system can be trusted under routine conditions, not just ideal ones.

In real work, reliability is what sustains use. Accuracy may attract attention, but reliability earns trust. Understanding the difference helps organizations design AI systems that endure beyond initial success and continue to support decisions in the long term.

The Hidden Work After the Demo

A successful AI demonstration often feels like a turning point. The system works. Outputs look sensible. Stakeholders are impressed. This moment creates the impression that the hardest work is done. In reality, it is where a different kind of work begins.

After the demo, AI systems must operate in real conditions. This requires ongoing attention that is rarely visible during early stages.

Behavior must be observed, not just celebrated. Small shifts in context can produce unexpected outcomes. Monitoring is not about watching for failure; it is about understanding how the system behaves over time.

Exceptions are another source of hidden work. No AI system handles every situation well. Edge cases emerge once the system is exposed to everyday use. People encounter scenarios that were not anticipated. Handling these cases requires judgment. Decisions must be made about when to override, when to adjust, and when to accept limitations. This work often falls to the same teams who built the system, extending their involvement indefinitely.

Maintaining trust requires constant care. Trust is built through consistent experience. It is damaged by surprises. When AI behavior changes without explanation, confidence declines. People become cautious or disengaged. Restoring trust is harder than building it initially. This makes communication and expectation management part of the system's ongoing operation.

There is also the work of alignment. As organizations change, so do priorities. AI systems must adapt or risk becoming irrelevant. This adaptation is not automatic. It requires revisiting objectives, reviewing usage patterns, and deciding whether the system still serves its intended purpose.

Much of this work is invisible because it does not produce new features or dramatic improvements. It produces stability. When done well, nothing appears to happen. When neglected, problems accumulate quietly.

The hidden work after the demo explains why many AI initiatives stall. Teams underestimate the effort required to sustain intelligence. The demo proves possibility. Ongoing work determines value.

Recognizing this reality changes how success is defined. It shifts focus from impressive moments to sustained usefulness. AI systems succeed not because they look intelligent once, but because they continue to support real work over time.

Humans Don't Trust Demos

Demos are designed to impress. They highlight best-case scenarios, smooth interactions, and confident outputs. In AI work, demonstrations often succeed at showing what a system can do. What they do not show is how the system behaves when conditions are less ideal. This gap explains why demos rarely create lasting trust.

Trust develops through experience, not exposure. People rely on systems that behave predictably across routine situations. An impressive demonstration may spark interest, but it does not answer the questions that matter in daily work. How often will this be useful? What happens when it is wrong? Who is responsible when outcomes are poor? These concerns cannot be resolved in a demo.

Human judgment plays a central role here. People assess trustworthiness over time by observing patterns. They notice consistency, responsiveness, and limits. AI systems that perform well occasionally but behave unpredictably undermine confidence. Even accurate outputs lose value when users are unsure how to act on them.

Accountability further shapes trust. In real work, decisions carry consequences. People want to know when they can rely on a system and when they should intervene. Demos rarely address this boundary. They focus on success, not responsibility. Without clarity, users hesitate to integrate AI into their decision-making.

Learning curves also matter. Trust in AI grows as people learn how the system fits into their work. This learning requires repeated interaction. Users need time to understand strengths and limitations. Demos compress this process into a single moment, creating unrealistic expectations.

Empathy is important in understanding this hesitation. Distrust is not resistance. It is a rational response to uncertainty. People protect themselves and their responsibilities. AI systems earn trust by respecting this instinct rather than trying to bypass it.

Over time, consistent behavior builds confidence. Small, reliable contributions matter more than dramatic results. When AI systems support decisions quietly and predictably, trust accumulates. When they surprise or overwhelm, trust erodes.

Recognizing that humans don't trust demos reframes success. It shifts focus from persuasion to reliability. AI systems that earn trust do so not by impressing once, but by showing up consistently in real work.

When POCs Delay Commitment

Proof-of-concept projects are often introduced as a responsible first step in AI work. They allow teams to explore possibilities without fully committing. Used carefully, they serve a purpose. Used repeatedly, they can become a way to avoid decisions rather than prepare for them.

AI POCs delay commitment by keeping responsibility optional. As long as a system is labeled experimental, no one has to own its outcomes. Decisions influenced by the system remain hypothetical. If results are promising, the project can continue. If results disappoint, it can be quietly set aside. This flexibility feels safe, but it prevents accountability from ever forming.

Organizations often remain in experimentation mode because it lowers risk in the short term. AI introduces uncertainty, and POCs contain that uncertainty. They allow learning without consequence. Over time, however, this caution becomes a pattern. Teams become skilled at building demonstrations and less experienced at deploying systems that change real work.

Repeated POCs also blur objectives. Each experiment explores a slightly different angle. Success criteria shift. What began as exploration becomes a series of disconnected efforts. Momentum exists, but direction does not. The organization moves, but it does not arrive anywhere.

Another reason POCs persist is that they align with existing incentives. Experiments produce visible artifacts, presentations, and updates. They signal activity and innovation without requiring structural change. Real deployment, by contrast, demands decisions about ownership, process, and risk. These decisions are harder and less rewarding in the short term.

The cost of prolonged experimentation is subtle. Trust stagnates because systems never prove themselves in real conditions. Learning remains incomplete because consequences are absent. People grow skeptical, not because AI fails, but because it never commits.

Commitment does not mean abandoning caution. It means deciding where intelligence will be used and who will stand behind it. Without this decision, AI remains an exercise rather than a capability.

Understanding when POCs delay commitment helps organizations move forward intentionally. Experiments should lead somewhere. When they do not, they protect the organization from risk at the expense of progress. Recognizing this trade-off is essential for turning potential into real work.

Designing for Life, Not the Lab

AI systems often look their best in controlled environments. Inputs are clean, scenarios are known, and expectations are carefully managed. In these conditions, intelligence appears stable and impressive. Real work, however, does not resemble a lab. It is messy, pressured, and shaped by human behavior. Designing AI for life requires a different mindset.

In real environments, conditions change continuously. Data shifts. Priorities evolve. People use systems in unexpected ways. AI systems must adapt to this variability without becoming unpredictable. This balance is difficult. Too rigid, and the system becomes irrelevant. Too flexible, and it becomes unreliable. Designing for life means accepting this tension rather than trying to eliminate it.

I have seen this difference clearly in financial institutions introducing AI for credit risk and fraud monitoring. In pilot environments, models performed well. Historical data was structured. Edge cases were filtered. Performance looked consistent. But once deployed into production, the behavior of the system changed—not because the model suddenly became weaker, but because reality introduced new variables. Economic conditions shifted. Customer behavior evolved. Regulatory scrutiny increased. Front-line teams interpreted outputs differently than analysts did in testing.

What looked stable in a controlled evaluation began interacting with human judgment, policy constraints, and operational pressure. The lab measured accuracy. Production revealed reliability.

Feedback plays a central role. In the lab, feedback is structured and intentional. In real work, it is uneven. Some signals are loud.

Others are silent. People may stop using a system without explaining why. In one case, analysts quietly reverted to manual review for certain borderline cases—not because the AI was wrong, but because its behavior under rare scenarios felt unpredictable. No formal complaint was raised. Usage patterns told the story.

Designing for life requires paying attention to these signals and treating them as information rather than noise.

Long-term use reveals patterns that short tests cannot. Initial enthusiasm fades. Habits form. Workarounds emerge. AI systems must survive this transition from novelty to routine. This requires humility in design. Systems should support gradual learning rather than assume immediate trust.

Adaptation over time also introduces responsibility. As systems change, expectations must be managed. Users need to understand what remains stable and what may evolve. Without this clarity, change feels like instability. In regulated environments especially, even minor behavioral shifts can create concern. Designing for life means making adaptation visible and understandable.

Designing for the lab optimizes for demonstration. Designing for life optimizes for endurance. The latter values consistency over perfection and clarity over cleverness. It recognizes that real value emerges slowly, through sustained use.

AI systems succeed when they fit into the rhythm of work rather than disrupting it. This fit cannot be proven in isolation. It is earned over time. Designing for life means accepting imperfection and focusing on long-term usefulness.

In real work, intelligence must live with people, processes, and change. Designing with this reality in mind is what allows AI systems to move beyond the lab and become part of everyday decision-making.

What Success Looks Like Beyond the POC

Beyond the proof of concept, success in AI looks quieter than many expect. There are fewer demonstrations and fewer moments of visible excitement. Instead, value shows up in small, consistent changes to how work is done. Decisions shift subtly. Confidence grows gradually. The system becomes part of the environment rather than the center of attention.

One sign of success is decision impact. AI outputs are no longer treated as interesting information. They influence choices in a repeatable way. People know when to consult the system and how its input fits into their judgment. The system does not need constant explanation. Its role is understood.

Trust is another indicator. Trust does not mean blind reliance. It means appropriate reliance. Users know the system's strengths and limits. They feel comfortable acting on its guidance when conditions are right and overriding it when they are not. This balance develops through experience, not instruction.

Stability matters more than novelty. Successful AI systems behave consistently over time. Changes are expected and explained. Surprises are rare. When behavior shifts, it does so within understood boundaries. This predictability allows people to integrate intelligence into their routines without hesitation.

In mature deployments, AI systems also recede into the background. They support work without demanding attention.

People stop talking about the technology and start talking about outcomes. This invisibility is a sign of success, not failure.

Beyond the POC, success is not measured by how advanced the system appears, but by how naturally it fits into real work. AI becomes useful not because it is impressive, but because it is dependable.

A Practical Test for POC Readiness

Knowing when an AI proof of concept is ready to move forward is often harder than starting it. POCs produce outputs, metrics, and demonstrations, but none of these automatically signal readiness for real use. Readiness is not about whether the system works in isolation. It is about whether the organization is prepared to live with its behavior.

One useful question is: Which decision will this AI system influence next week, and who will be responsible for acting on it? This question forces specificity. If the answer remains hypothetical—it could help with…, it might support…—the POC is not ready. AI becomes meaningful only when someone is prepared to change a decision because of it. Without that commitment, moving toward production simply extends experimentation.

This question also reveals ownership. If responsibility shifts or feels uncomfortable, that discomfort is informative. It signals that the system's role is still unclear. Promoting such a POC introduces intelligence without accountability, a common cause of failure later.

A second question is: What happens when the AI behaves unexpectedly?
This tests operational readiness. In real work, AI systems will

produce surprising or imperfect outputs. If there is no agreed response—who reviews, who overrides, who explains—the system is not ready for broader use. Production environments demand predictable handling of uncertainty, not just impressive behavior.

These questions expose whether the organization has moved beyond curiosity. They shift attention from what the system can do to how it will be used, trusted, and managed. They also prevent premature escalation. A POC that performs well but lacks operational grounding is fragile.

Readiness does not require certainty. It requires preparedness. When teams can answer these questions clearly and consistently, they signal that intelligence has a place in real work. When they cannot, the most responsible choice is to pause.

Using simple tests like these keeps AI efforts honest. They help organizations transition from demonstration to commitment thoughtfully, ensuring that when intelligence moves forward, it does so with clarity rather than hope.

Working Is Not Enough

In AI work, it is easy to mistake functionality for success. When a system produces outputs and behaves as expected in isolation, it is often described as working. Yet working is only the beginning. AI creates value only when it is trusted, used, and sustained over time.

Trust cannot be assumed. It develops through consistent experience in real conditions. People learn whether a system fits their judgment, respects their responsibilities, and behaves within understood limits. Without this trust, even capable systems remain on the sidelines. They exist, but they do not influence decisions.

Use is equally critical. AI systems must integrate into daily work in a way that feels natural rather than disruptive. If intelligence requires constant explanation or special handling, it becomes optional. Optional systems are rarely relied upon. Use emerges when people understand when and how the system should inform their choices.

Sustainment is often overlooked. AI systems demand ongoing attention. They must be observed, adjusted, and sometimes constrained. This work is not glamorous, but it determines longevity. Systems that are not sustained gradually lose relevance, even if they once performed well.

These three elements—trust, use, and sustainment—are what turn intelligence into impact. Without them, AI remains a technical artifact rather than a practical capability.

As this chapter closes, the distinction becomes clear. A system that works in a demo proves possibility. A system that works in real life proves judgment. The difference lies not in sophistication, but in how intelligence is treated over time.

The next chapter shifts focus to design and structure. It explores how architectural and thinking choices shape whether AI systems can be trusted, used, and sustained. Working is not enough. What matters is whether intelligence becomes part of real work.

Chapter 6
Architecture Reflects Thinking

Architecture Is a Mirror

AI systems are often described in terms of their components, layers, or technical choices. Yet beneath these details lies something more revealing. The structure of an AI system reflects how an organization thinks. Architecture is not neutral. It is a mirror of assumptions about decisions, uncertainty, and responsibility.

When thinking is clear, architecture tends to be simple. The system is designed around a specific decision. Boundaries are explicit. Roles are understood. Intelligence appears where it is needed and stops where human judgment should remain. This restraint is visible in how the system is shaped. It does not attempt to do everything. It does one thing well.

When thinking is unclear, architecture becomes complicated. Systems accumulate capabilities to satisfy multiple, sometimes conflicting interpretations of purpose. Intelligence is added broadly rather than precisely. Outputs multiply because no single decision anchors the design. The architecture reflects hesitation. It tries to cover uncertainty instead of confronting it.

AI makes these patterns more visible than traditional software. Because AI operates under uncertainty, architectural choices signal how that uncertainty is managed. Where does interpretation happen? Who decides when to act? How are exceptions handled? These questions are answered implicitly through structure, even when they are not discussed explicitly.

Responsibility is also embedded in architecture. If outputs flow freely without clear handoffs, accountability becomes diffuse. If override mechanisms are unclear, people hesitate. The system may function, but no one feels comfortable relying on it. This discomfort is not a technical issue. It is a design consequence of unresolved responsibility.

Architecture also reveals attitudes toward trust. Systems designed to be overly protective often reflect fear of error. Systems designed with no constraints often reflect overconfidence. Balanced architecture acknowledges uncertainty without being paralyzed by it. It creates space for learning while maintaining stability.

Importantly, architecture outlives intent. Initial objectives may be forgotten, but structure remains. Over time, people adapt to the system as it is, not as it was meant to be. If assumptions were flawed, those flaws become institutionalized through architecture.

Seeing architecture as a mirror changes how AI systems are discussed. It shifts attention from what is built to why it is built that way. It encourages teams to examine their own thinking before refining structure.

In AI work, architecture is not just a technical outcome. It is a record of decisions made and decisions avoided. Reading it carefully reveals whether intelligence is being used with clarity or as a substitute for it.

Complexity Often Hides Confusion

In AI systems, complexity is frequently mistaken for sophistication. Layers are added, pathways multiply, and behavior becomes harder to explain. From the outside, this complexity can look like progress. From the inside, it often signals something else: unresolved confusion about purpose and decisions.

When objectives are unclear, teams compensate by expanding scope. Rather than deciding what the system should influence, they try to make it adaptable to many possibilities. Intelligence is spread across multiple functions in the hope that value will emerge somewhere. This approach feels cautious, but it produces systems that are difficult to reason about and harder to trust.

AI's inherent uncertainty plays a role in this pattern. Because outputs are probabilistic, teams may respond by adding layers of checks, alternatives, or fallbacks. Each layer addresses a specific concern, but together they obscure the original intent. The system grows not from clarity, but from accumulated hesitation.

Complexity also emerges when decision paths are undefined. If it is unclear who should act on an output, the system is often designed to serve multiple audiences. Information is packaged in different forms for different users. What begins as flexibility becomes fragmentation. No single path feels authoritative, and responsibility remains diffuse.

This layering creates operational burden. More complexity requires more explanation, more maintenance, and more interpretation. Users must learn not only what the system does, but how to navigate it. Over time, this effort erodes confidence. People rely on simpler cues or bypass the system entirely.

Importantly, complexity can delay difficult conversations. Adding structure feels productive. Clarifying decisions requires agreement.

When alignment is hard, complexity becomes a substitute. The system absorbs ambiguity instead of resolving it. AI amplifies this effect because it can operate under many interpretations without immediate failure.

The cost of this approach becomes visible in production. Complex systems are fragile. Small changes have unpredictable effects. Diagnosing issues takes longer because cause and effect are obscured. What was meant to manage uncertainty ends up increasing it.

Simplicity, by contrast, is a result of clarity. When objectives and decision paths are explicit, architecture can be restrained. Intelligence is placed deliberately. Boundaries are respected. The system becomes easier to understand and easier to evolve.

Recognizing that complexity often hides confusion invites a different response. Instead of asking how to manage complexity, teams can ask why it exists. In AI work, reducing complexity is rarely a technical exercise. It is an act of clarification.

Boundaries Matter More in AI Systems

All systems benefit from clear boundaries, but in AI work they are especially important. Intelligence introduces uncertainty, change, and learning behavior. Without clear limits, these qualities spread in ways that are difficult to control. Boundaries define where intelligence should operate and where it should stop.

AI systems learn from patterns in their environment. When boundaries are vague, learning behavior can drift. The system begins to respond to signals that were never intended to influence it. This drift is often subtle. It does not trigger obvious failure, but it gradually changes how the system behaves. Clear boundaries constrain learning to what matters.

Uncertainty makes boundaries necessary for trust. People need to know what an AI system is responsible for and what it is not. When outputs appear outside expected scope, confidence erodes. Users hesitate because they cannot predict when the system should be relied upon. Boundaries create expectation. They make behavior understandable even when outcomes vary.

Evolving inputs add another challenge. Real environments change. New situations arise. Without boundaries, AI systems may attempt to adapt to everything. This adaptability seems powerful, but it increases risk. Systems become harder to reason about because their role is not fixed. Boundaries allow adaptation within a defined purpose rather than across an undefined space.

Boundaries also support responsibility. When it is clear where the system's influence ends, ownership begins. People know when to step in and when to defer. This clarity reduces hesitation and over-reliance. It makes collaboration between humans and intelligence possible.

In practice, missing boundaries often show up as confusion. Users ask whether a system applies in a particular case. Teams debate whether an output should be acted upon. These questions indicate that the system's role was never fully defined. Intelligence fills the gap, but not reliably.

Clear boundaries do not limit value. They protect it. By defining what the system will not do, teams make what it does more trustworthy. AI systems with clear boundaries are easier to explain, easier to maintain, and easier to integrate into real work.

In AI design, boundaries are not constraints to be minimized. They are commitments to clarity. They ensure that intelligence supports decisions without overrunning them.

Where Decisions Live in the Architecture

In AI systems, decisions are always being made, whether or not they are acknowledged explicitly. Architecture determines where those decisions live. It reveals whether choices are owned by people, embedded in systems, or lost in unclear handoffs between the two.

When decisions live clearly with humans, AI acts as a support mechanism. The system surfaces signals, patterns, or suggestions, but judgment remains visible. Architecture in these cases makes the moment of decision explicit. People know when they are expected to interpret outputs, weigh context, and take responsibility for action. This clarity supports both trust and accountability.

In large financial institutions, this distinction becomes critical. I have seen credit risk systems deployed in cloud environments where models ran flawlessly, pipelines were stable, and monitoring dashboards were elegant—yet confusion remained about one simple question: who ultimately approves the borderline cases? The architecture defined data flow and model execution precisely, but the decision checkpoint was vague. Relationship managers assumed risk teams would review. Risk teams assumed the model threshold was final. The system was technically sound, but architecturally ambiguous. The problem was not model accuracy. It was that the architecture had not clearly declared where the human decision lived.

In other cases, decisions are quietly embedded inside systems. Outputs trigger actions automatically or shape outcomes without a clear human checkpoint. This design can be appropriate in narrow, low-risk contexts, but it carries consequences. Responsibility becomes harder to trace. When results are poor, it is unclear whether the system's behavior or human oversight should be questioned. Over time, this ambiguity weakens confidence.

The most fragile situation occurs when decisions live nowhere clearly. AI produces outputs, but no one is sure who should act on them. Systems assume people will decide. People assume the system is authoritative. The architecture does not resolve this tension. Instead, it hides it. The result is hesitation, inconsistency, or silent avoidance.

These unclear handoffs are common in AI initiatives. Intelligence is added without redesigning decision flow. Outputs are delivered, but ownership is never fully assigned. Architecture reflects this avoidance by spreading responsibility thinly rather than placing it deliberately.

Hiding decisions inside systems also removes opportunities for reflection. When judgment is embedded implicitly, it becomes harder to question. People stop asking why a decision was made and start focusing only on outcomes. When errors occur, diagnosis becomes difficult because the decision path is opaque. The architecture does not reveal where reasoning happened or where assumptions entered.

Clear architectures do the opposite. They make decision points visible. They show when AI informs, when it recommends, and when it intervenes. They define where responsibility shifts and where it remains firmly human. This visibility allows organizations to learn, adjust, and improve over time.

In AI work, architecture is not just structural. t is operational and accountable. Where decisions live determines who answers for outcomes. When architecture hides this reality, systems may appear efficient but become brittle. When it exposes it, intelligence can be used confidently and responsibly.

Designing with decision location in mind ensures that AI strengthens judgment rather than replacing it unintentionally. It allows intelligence to support real work without obscuring accountability. That clarity is what allows AI systems to endure beyond initial success.

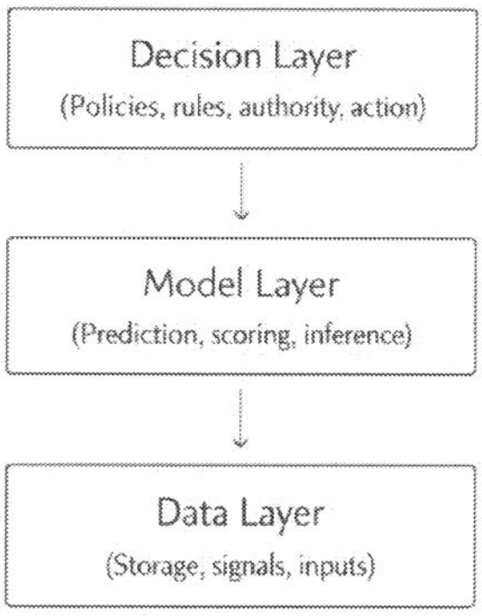

Figure 5. Decision-Led AI Architecture

Although data flows upward during execution, architecture should be designed downward from decisions.

Designing for Change, Not Perfection

AI systems are often introduced with a quiet assumption: if they are accurate enough at the start, they will remain useful over time. This assumption drives teams to focus heavily on initial performance. Effort is spent refining behavior, reducing errors, and polishing outputs before the system ever meets real work. While this attention feels responsible, it misunderstands what makes AI systems endure.

AI systems do not operate in fixed environments. They interact with changing conditions, evolving inputs, and human behavior that adapts in response to the system itself. What appears accurate today may behave differently tomorrow. Designing for perfection at the outset ignores this reality. It treats intelligence as static when it is inherently dynamic.

Learning behavior is central to this challenge. AI systems adjust as patterns shift and feedback accumulates. This ability to learn is often described as their greatest strength, but it also introduces instability if not designed for thoughtfully. Systems that are optimized narrowly for initial conditions can become brittle. Small changes in context produce unexpected behavior because adaptation was not anticipated.

Designing for change means accepting that behavior will evolve. It requires making that evolution visible rather than hiding it. People need to understand that intelligence is not fixed and that adjustments are part of normal operation. When change is expected, it is easier to manage. When it arrives unexpectedly, trust erodes.

Feedback plays a crucial role in this design approach. AI systems depend on feedback to remain aligned with their purpose. Without clear channels for learning from use, systems drift away from intended outcomes. Designing for change means treating feedback as a first-class element of the system, not as an afterthought. It acknowledges that real-world use is the primary source of learning.

Adaptation also has implications for responsibility. When systems change, someone must notice, interpret, and decide whether adjustment is appropriate. Designing for change makes these responsibilities explicit. It avoids the illusion that intelligence can manage itself indefinitely. AI systems require stewardship, not just deployment.

Perfection-focused design often aims to minimize the need for intervention. Change-focused design accepts intervention as inevitable. This acceptance leads to architectures that are more resilient because they are built around ongoing attention rather than one-time success.

Importantly, designing for change does not mean accepting instability. It means defining where change is allowed and where consistency must be preserved. Boundaries remain essential. Adaptation occurs within purpose, not across it.

In real work, value emerges over time. AI systems that endure are not those that perform best on day one, but those that remain useful as conditions evolve. Designing for change rather than perfection aligns intelligence with reality. It prepares systems to live alongside people, processes, and uncertainty without losing their role or their trust.

Human Roles Shape Architecture

AI architecture is often discussed as a technical construct, but its shape is deeply influenced by assumptions about people. Every design choice reflects beliefs about who will judge, who will oversee, and who will be responsible when outcomes matter. Whether these assumptions are explicit or implicit, they determine how intelligence is integrated into real work.

When human roles are clear, architecture follows suit. Systems are designed with defined moments for interpretation, review, and action. AI provides input where it adds value, and humans retain authority where judgment is required. These systems feel intentional. People understand their role in relation to the system and trust grows because responsibility is visible.

Clear human roles also simplify structure. When it is known who decides and who oversees, the system does not need to compensate for uncertainty. It does not attempt to guide every scenario or cover every edge case. Architecture becomes restrained, focusing on supporting specific decisions rather than managing ambiguity.

By contrast, ambiguous human roles produce complex architectures. When it is unclear who is expected to act on AI outputs, systems are often designed to do more. Intelligence is added broadly in an attempt to reduce reliance on human judgment. This approach shifts responsibility without resolving it. The architecture becomes heavier as it tries to replace clarity with capability.

Ambiguity also leads to defensive design. Systems are built with multiple layers of checks or signals because no one is sure where oversight should occur. Each layer addresses a perceived risk, but together they obscure accountability. People hesitate because they do not know when they are meant to intervene or defer.

Assumptions about trust further shape architecture. If designers believe humans cannot be trusted to make consistent decisions, systems may be built to automate aggressively. If they believe people will resist automation, systems may be overly cautious. Both assumptions influence structure. In either case, architecture reflects beliefs about human reliability rather than observed behavior.

Responsibility is another critical factor. When accountability is unclear, architecture often hides decisions. Outputs flow without clear ownership, allowing action to occur without explicit commitment. This design reduces friction in the short term but creates risk over time. When outcomes disappoint, it is difficult to identify where judgment failed.

Systems designed with clear human roles handle uncertainty more effectively. They acknowledge that intelligence supports judgment rather than replacing it. Architecture in these cases makes room for learning and adaptation without losing sight of responsibility.

Ultimately, AI architecture is shaped less by technology than by organizational beliefs about people. When those beliefs are realistic and explicit, systems become simpler and more trustworthy. When they are vague or conflicted, complexity grows.

Recognizing that human roles shape architecture invites a different design conversation. It encourages teams to clarify responsibility before adding intelligence. In AI work, clarity about people is what allows structure to serve decisions rather than obscure them.

Over-Engineering Is Often Fear

Over-engineering in AI systems is rarely the result of ambition alone. More often, it is a response to discomfort. When uncertainty feels threatening and responsibility is unclear, complexity becomes a form of protection. Additional layers, checks, and capabilities offer the illusion of control, even when they do not improve outcomes.

AI introduces a particular kind of uncertainty. Its outputs are probabilistic. Its behavior can change over time. Its influence depends on how people interpret and act on its signals. These qualities make it harder to feel confident about decisions. When that confidence is missing, teams often respond by adding more intelligence rather than clarifying intent.

Fear shows up subtly. A system is asked to handle more scenarios than originally intended, just in case. Extra safeguards are introduced to cover unlikely situations. Multiple outputs are provided so users can choose what feels right. Each addition seems reasonable on its own. Together, they create a system that is harder to understand and harder to trust.

Risk avoidance plays a role as well. When no one wants to be responsible for a wrong decision, architecture expands to distribute perceived risk. Intelligence is layered so that no single output feels decisive. Responsibility is diffused across the system. This design reduces immediate pressure, but it also reduces clarity. Decisions become harder, not easier.

Over-engineering is also a response to unclear decision paths. When it is not clear which decision the system should influence, teams design for flexibility. Intelligence is spread broadly to remain useful under multiple interpretations. The system becomes capable of many things but accountable for none.

AI-specific uncertainty amplifies this pattern. Because behavior can evolve, teams worry about what might happen later. Instead of defining boundaries, they attempt to anticipate every possibility. The result is architecture built around hypothetical risks rather than real needs.

The cost of this approach emerges slowly. Complex systems demand more explanation. Users must interpret not only outputs but also which outputs matter. Over time, confidence erodes. People simplify by ignoring parts of the system or relying on intuition instead. The very complexity meant to reduce risk ends up undermining value.

Recognizing fear as a driver of over-engineering is not an accusation. It is an invitation to reflect. Fear often signals unresolved questions about purpose, ownership, or trust. Addressing those questions directly reduces the need for architectural compensation.

In mature AI work, simplicity is not naive. It is deliberate. It reflects decisions that have been made and responsibilities that are accepted. Over-engineering fades when clarity replaces fear. Intelligence becomes lighter, more focused, and more useful—not because it does less, but because it does what matters.

What Simple AI Architectures Have in Common

Simple AI architectures are often misunderstood. They are not simple because the problems they address are easy, nor because the organizations using them lack ambition. They are simple because the thinking behind them is clear. Across different contexts, effective and restrained AI systems tend to share a small set of common patterns.

The first is clarity of purpose. Simple architectures are built around a specific decision, not a general capability. They exist to influence a defined moment in work. Because this purpose is explicit, the system does not need to stretch beyond it. Intelligence is applied narrowly and intentionally. This focus reduces ambiguity and makes the system easier to trust.

Stability is another shared trait. Simple AI systems behave consistently within known boundaries. They do not attempt to adapt to everything. Instead, they adapt where it matters and remain predictable elsewhere. This balance helps users form reliable expectations. When behavior is stable, people feel more confident integrating intelligence into their routines.

Decision alignment is equally important. In simple architectures, it is clear how outputs relate to actions. People understand when the system's input should be considered and how it fits into judgment.

There is little confusion about ownership. The system does not compete with human decision-making; it supports it.

Effective systems also make uncertainty visible without amplifying it. They acknowledge that AI outputs are not definitive, but they do not overwhelm users with options or signals. By limiting scope, they reduce the cognitive burden of interpretation. Users spend less time questioning the system and more time using it.

Another common pattern is restraint in change. Simple architectures are designed to evolve slowly and deliberately. Adjustments are made in response to observed behavior, not hypothetical scenarios. This measured approach preserves trust and prevents instability.

Finally, simple AI systems respect human roles. They are designed with realistic assumptions about attention, judgment, and responsibility. They do not attempt to replace what humans do well. Instead, they complement existing strengths. This respect shows up in how intelligence is integrated rather than imposed.

Together, these patterns explain why simplicity works. It is not about minimizing capability. It is about maximizing usefulness. Simple AI architectures endure because they are understandable, dependable, and aligned with real decisions. They demonstrate that clarity, not complexity, is what allows intelligence to create lasting value.

A Question to Ask of Any AI Architecture

When AI architectures become complex, it is often hard to tell whether that complexity serves a purpose or simply manages uncertainty. Diagrams grow. Responsibilities blur. Decisions are discussed, but rarely named. In these moments, a single question can cut through noise and reveal what the architecture is really doing.

The question is this: If this AI system disappeared tomorrow, which decision would immediately revert to a human—and who would notice first?

This question works because it forces specificity. If no clear decision comes to mind, the architecture is likely managing complexity rather than supporting real work. Intelligence may be present, but it is not anchored to action. Outputs exist, but they are not essential.

Asking who would notice first matters just as much. It exposes ownership. If the answer is vague—someone in operations, the business, the users—responsibility is diffuse. AI systems in this state often survive because they appear useful, not because they are relied upon. Their absence would be inconvenient, but not consequential.

In contrast, architectures that support real decisions produce clear answers. A specific role would feel the loss. A known decision would slow down, change, or require manual handling. This clarity signals that intelligence is integrated into work rather than layered on top of it.

Using this question in practice is straightforward. It can be asked during design discussions, before scaling, or when systems feel heavier than expected. The goal is not to justify the architecture, but to understand it. Honest answers are more valuable than reassuring ones.

If the question reveals weak decision linkage, the response should not be to add more intelligence. It should be to clarify purpose. What decision is meant to change? Where should judgment live?

Simplifying architecture often begins with answering these questions, not with redesigning structure.

This question also helps teams recognize when AI is being used defensively. Architectures built to avoid responsibility often struggle to answer who would notice first. Intelligence exists, but no one depends on it enough to feel its absence. That dependency gap is a design signal, not a usage problem.

Over time, regularly asking this question builds discipline. It keeps architecture aligned with decisions as conditions evolve. It prevents systems from drifting into complexity without consequence.

AI architectures earn their place by supporting decisions that matter. When this question has a clear, confident answer, architecture is likely doing its job. When it does not, the system may be impressive—but not essential.

Structure Follows Thought

AI architecture is often treated as a technical artifact, something that can be refined independently of how people think or decide. In practice, structure follows thought. The shape of an AI system reflects how clearly decisions are understood, how uncertainty is tolerated, and how responsibility is distributed.

When thinking is precise, structure becomes restrained. Systems are designed around known decisions and explicit boundaries. Intelligence appears where it is useful and stops where judgment must remain human. This clarity produces architectures that feel calm. They are easier to explain, easier to trust, and easier to live with over time.

When thinking is unresolved, structure compensates. Architecture expands to absorb ambiguity. Intelligence is added to manage uncertainty rather than confront it. Responsibility is diffused through layers rather than assigned deliberately. The system may function, but it carries the tension of unanswered questions within its design.

AI makes this relationship visible because it operates under uncertainty by default. Its behavior forces organizations to confront how much variability they are willing to accept and who will answer for outcomes. Architecture records those answers, even when they are never spoken aloud.

This is why redesigning structure without revisiting thinking rarely works. Complexity does not disappear when it is reorganized. It disappears when purpose becomes clearer. Architecture simplifies naturally when decisions are named and ownership is accepted.

Seeing structure as an outcome of thought changes how AI systems are evaluated. Instead of asking whether the architecture is sophisticated, the more useful question becomes whether it is honest. Does it reflect clarity, or does it hide hesitation? Does it surface responsibility, or does it diffuse it?

As this chapter closes, one idea remains: AI architecture is not where clarity is created. It is where clarity is revealed. Systems look the way they do because of the decisions that were made—or avoided—along the way.

The next chapter turns to trust and adoption. It explores how people learn to rely on AI systems once they are in place, and how confidence grows or erodes through use. Structure sets the stage. Trust determines whether intelligence becomes part of real work.

Chapter 7
Trust as the Real Constraint

Trust, Not Accuracy, Limits AI

AI systems often reach a level of technical performance that appears sufficient for real use. Outputs are sensible. Behavior is consistent under testing. From a technical perspective, the system works. Yet in many organizations, these systems remain peripheral. Decisions continue as before. The limitation is not accuracy. It is trust.

Trust in AI is shaped by uncertainty. Unlike deterministic systems, AI produces probabilistic outputs. Even when results are usually correct, they are rarely definitive. This uncertainty requires interpretation. People must decide when to rely on the system and when to question it. That judgment introduces hesitation, especially when consequences matter.

Human hesitation is not resistance. It is a rational response to responsibility. When decisions carry risk, people want to understand not just what the system suggests, but why. AI systems often struggle to provide explanations that feel intuitive or complete. As a result, users may accept outputs intellectually while remaining reluctant to act on them.

Trust is also influenced by consistency over time. An AI system may perform well most of the time and still lose credibility through occasional surprises. These moments linger in memory. They shape perception more than routine success. People adjust their behavior cautiously, reducing reliance even when overall performance remains strong.

Another factor is alignment with decision context. An accurate output delivered at the wrong moment or in the wrong form fails to build trust. AI systems must fit the rhythm of work. When they interrupt rather than support judgment, their influence diminishes. Trust grows when intelligence feels helpful, not intrusive.

Trust is fragile because it is experiential. It develops through repeated interaction, not demonstration. Early expectations matter. If AI is introduced as authoritative, disappointment follows when uncertainty appears. If it is framed as support, learning can occur. How systems are positioned shapes how they are trusted.

Importantly, trust is shared. It is not only about the system, but about the environment around it. Clear ownership, stable processes, and visible responsibility make it easier to rely on intelligence. Without these conditions, even accurate systems struggle to matter.

This explains why improving performance alone often fails to change outcomes. Accuracy attracts attention. Trust sustains use. In real work, decisions are shaped by confidence, accountability, and experience. AI systems influence decisions only when they earn a place within that human framework.

Understanding that trust, not accuracy, limits AI shifts the focus of design and deployment. It encourages patience over persuasion and consistency over spectacle. AI succeeds not by convincing people once, but by supporting them reliably over time.

How Humans Learn to Trust AI

Trust in AI does not emerge from instruction or persuasion. It develops the same way trust in any system does: through experience. People learn whether an AI system deserves reliance by observing how it behaves over time, especially when conditions are imperfect.

Repeated exposure is the foundation. The first interactions with an AI system are rarely decisive. Users are cautious. They test boundaries quietly. They compare outputs with their own judgment. Over time, patterns emerge. If the system behaves consistently in familiar situations, confidence grows. If it behaves unpredictably, hesitation hardens into avoidance.

Consistency matters more than occasional brilliance. A system that is helpful most days earns more trust than one that is impressive once. Humans value reliability because it reduces cognitive load. When people know what to expect, they can focus on decisions rather than second-guessing the system.

Understanding limitations accelerates trust rather than weakening it. When users know where an AI system performs well and where it does not, they adjust their expectations. Surprise is minimized. Errors become tolerable because they occur within understood boundaries. Trust erodes not because systems fail, but because failures violate expectation.

Learning also happens through contrast. People notice when AI improves their work and when it does not. They observe whether it saves time, reduces uncertainty, or clarifies choices. These moments accumulate quietly. Over time, reliance becomes habitual. The system is consulted not because it is mandated, but because it has proven useful.

Human learning is social as well. Trust spreads through shared experience. When colleagues reference an AI system naturally, others follow. When skepticism circulates, adoption slows. These dynamics cannot be engineered directly. They emerge from lived interaction.

Importantly, trust develops when people feel permitted to disagree with the system. AI that demands obedience creates resistance. AI that invites judgment fosters learning. When users know they can override outputs without consequence, they engage more openly. This engagement is what builds familiarity and confidence.

Learning to trust AI is not about convincing people that systems are correct. It is about helping them understand how to work with uncertainty. Over time, users learn when to lean on intelligence and when to rely on themselves. That balance is where trust lives.

In real work, trust is earned incrementally. It grows through consistent behavior, visible limits, and respectful integration into human judgment. AI systems that recognize this learning process do not rush adoption. They allow trust to form naturally, one interaction at a time.

The First Failure Matters Too Much

The first failure of an AI system carries more weight than it should. Long before a system has established a track record, an early mistake can shape perception permanently. Adoption slows. Confidence weakens. Even when performance improves later, hesitation remains. This disproportionate impact is not a technical problem. It is a human one.

Early expectations play a critical role. AI systems are often introduced with an implicit promise of intelligence. Outputs appear thoughtful. Language feels confident. This creates an assumption of competence that exceeds reality. When the first visible failure occurs, it violates that assumption. The disappointment is sharper because the perceived intelligence was higher.

I have seen this pattern clearly in banking environments. A credit risk model was introduced to assist analysts with approval decisions. In testing, performance looked strong. In early production, it correctly flagged several risky applications that manual review had missed. Confidence grew quickly. Then, within the first few weeks, it incorrectly classified a well-qualified customer as high risk due to an unusual income structure. The error was caught and corrected. Financially, the impact was small. Perceptually, it was not.

From that point forward, analysts double-checked nearly every recommendation. Not because the system had become worse, but because its first visible failure had altered the mental model. The system was no longer "intelligent support." It was "potentially wrong." That shift happened faster than any performance metric could compensate for.

Humans are particularly sensitive to confidence collapse. When a system presents itself as capable and then behaves unexpectedly, people recalibrate quickly. They become cautious. They reduce reliance. The system may still be useful, but it is no longer trusted. That shift is difficult to reverse.

First failures also lack context. Users have not yet learned the system's limits. They do not know whether an error is rare or common. Without experience, they assume the worst. A single mistake stands in for an unknown pattern. This uncertainty amplifies the impact of early missteps.

AI-specific uncertainty intensifies this effect. Because behavior can change over time, users worry that failures may recur unpredictably. Even if the system performs well later, the memory of early failure lingers. People adjust behavior defensively, often choosing manual judgment over intelligence.

Perceived intelligence adds another layer. When AI outputs resemble human reasoning, errors feel more personal. Users feel misled rather than merely inconvenienced. This emotional response slows recovery. Trust is not withdrawn gradually; it collapses.

Organizations often underestimate this dynamic. They focus on improving performance after initial deployment, assuming trust will follow. In reality, early experiences dominate perception. Once confidence is lost, improvements are met with skepticism rather than relief.

This does not mean AI systems must be perfect at launch. It means expectations must be managed carefully. Introducing systems as support rather than authority reduces the shock of early failure. Allowing room for learning helps users contextualize mistakes.

Understanding that the first failure matters too much encourages restraint and patience. It shifts attention from technical readiness to experiential readiness. In AI adoption, the first impression is not about accuracy. It is about credibility. Protecting that credibility early determines whether intelligence earns a place in real work.

Trust Is Contextual, Not Global

Organizations often speak about "trusting AI" as if trust were a single switch that can be turned on or off. In practice, trust is contextual. It varies by decision type, level of risk, and the consequences attached to outcomes. Expecting universal trust from a system is unrealistic and often counterproductive.

Different decisions carry different stakes. When AI supports low-risk, reversible choices, people are more willing to rely on it. If the system suggests a minor adjustment or highlights a non-critical pattern, the cost of being wrong is limited. Trust grows more easily in these environments because consequences are manageable.

High-stakes decisions are different. When outcomes affect finances, safety, reputation, or long-term strategy, hesitation increases. Even technically strong systems are treated cautiously. Users seek additional validation. They ask more questions. This does not indicate distrust of the technology itself. It reflects the weight of responsibility attached to the decision.

I have seen this contrast clearly across industries. In an energy environment, an AI system was used to optimize maintenance scheduling for equipment. If a recommendation was slightly off, the impact was operational and correctable. Engineers gradually trusted the system because errors were visible, contained, and reversible. Trust grew through experience.

In a healthcare context, however, the same level of tolerance did not exist. When AI was used to assist in identifying potential diagnostic risks, even small inconsistencies created discomfort. Clinicians did not treat outputs as optimization suggestions; they treated them as inputs into life-impacting decisions. The system could be statistically sound, but trust remained conditional. The context demanded it.

Context also shapes perception inside the same organization. An AI system may be trusted in one department and questioned in another. Teams with direct experience and familiarity often develop confidence through use. Those observing from a distance may remain skeptical. Trust emerges from interaction, not from abstract reputation.

Risk tolerance further influences reliance. Some roles are structured around caution and compliance. Others prioritize speed and experimentation. The same AI output can be embraced in one setting and resisted in another. Architecture alone cannot solve this variation. It must be acknowledged as part of human judgment.

Unrealistic expectations arise when organizations assume that once AI performs well, it should be trusted everywhere. This assumption ignores the layered nature of trust. Confidence built in one context does not automatically transfer to another. A system that supports routine decisions effectively may still require human oversight in exceptional cases.

Recognizing contextual trust changes how AI is introduced. Rather than seeking universal acceptance, mature organizations define where trust should be highest and where it should remain conditional. They design systems with differentiated roles, allowing confidence to grow appropriately.

Contextual trust is not a weakness. It reflects discernment. It ensures that intelligence is used proportionately to risk. When expectations align with context, adoption becomes steadier and more sustainable.

AI systems earn trust incrementally within specific domains. Attempting to generalize that trust too broadly undermines it. Understanding this distinction helps organizations move beyond binary thinking and toward calibrated reliance.

In real work, trust is not global approval. It is contextual confidence. Recognizing this nuance allows AI to support decisions where it fits naturally, while preserving judgment where consequences demand it.

Explainability Is About Responsibility

Explainability in AI is often framed as a technical feature. Can the system justify its output? Can it show how it arrived at a conclusion? These questions matter, but they miss a deeper point. In real work, explanations are not primarily about satisfying curiosity. They are about clarifying responsibility.

When an AI system influences a decision, someone remains accountable for the outcome. That accountability does not disappear because intelligence was involved. Explanations help the responsible person understand what they are endorsing. Without that understanding, ownership becomes fragile.

Consider what happens when a system produces a recommendation without context. A user sees the output but does not grasp the reasoning behind it. Acting on that recommendation feels risky. If the outcome is poor, it is difficult to defend the choice. The absence of explanation shifts the burden entirely onto the human decision-maker, increasing hesitation.

Explainability supports judgment by making the boundaries of the system visible. It helps users see what factors were considered and, just as importantly, what was not. This clarity allows them to assess whether the recommendation fits the situation. The goal is not to replicate the system's internal logic in detail. It is to provide enough understanding for responsible action.

Responsibility also requires traceability. When outcomes are questioned, organizations need to understand how decisions were influenced. Explanations provide a path for reflection. They allow teams to learn from errors and refine systems. Without them, mistakes appear arbitrary. Trust erodes because there is no visible reasoning to evaluate.

Importantly, explainability should match context. Not every decision requires deep analysis. For routine, low-risk choices, simple clarity may suffice. For high-stakes decisions, more structured explanation becomes essential. The level of explanation needed is tied to the level of responsibility carried.

There is a misconception that explainability is about making AI feel transparent. In practice, it is about making accountability workable. People do not need to understand every detail. They need to understand enough to stand behind a decision.

Explainability also shapes trust. When users feel that they can question and understand outputs, they engage more confidently. The system becomes a partner in reasoning rather than a black box issuing instructions.

In mature AI use, explanations are designed alongside decisions. They are not added afterward. They reflect an understanding that intelligence does not remove responsibility. It redistributes it.

Seen this way, explainability is less a technical challenge and more an organizational commitment. It acknowledges that decisions matter and that those who make them deserve clarity. AI systems that respect this principle support responsible action rather than undermining it.

Trust Erodes Quietly

Trust in AI rarely collapses in a single dramatic moment. More often, it fades quietly. A small inconsistency here. An unexpected output there. A subtle change in behavior that no one fully understands. Each instance seems minor on its own. Over time, they accumulate.

AI systems operate under uncertainty. Their outputs are influenced by patterns that may shift gradually. This means behavior can change in ways that are technically reasonable but experientially unsettling. A recommendation that once appeared stable begins to fluctuate slightly. A prediction that felt dependable starts to feel less consistent. Users may not be able to articulate what changed, but they sense it.

Surprises are especially damaging. When an AI system behaves outside its perceived boundaries, even once, confidence weakens. If the system was expected to support routine decisions and suddenly produces an outlier, users hesitate the next time. They begin to double-check. The system moves from being relied upon to being verified.

Small inconsistencies have a similar effect. Perhaps the output format changes subtly. Perhaps similar situations receive slightly different recommendations. Individually, these differences may not be significant. Collectively, they signal instability. Users respond by lowering reliance.

Unclear behavior accelerates this erosion. If users cannot understand why a change occurred, they attribute it to unreliability. Even when performance remains strong, opacity breeds caution. People prefer systems that behave predictably within known limits.

Trust erodes quietly because it is rarely measured directly. Organizations track performance, not perception. A system may continue to perform well technically while users gradually disengage. They consult it less often. They rely on it only when convenient. Eventually, it becomes peripheral without anyone declaring it so.

This gradual decline is difficult to reverse. Once habits shift away from reliance, rebuilding confidence requires consistent positive experience over time. Dramatic improvements rarely restore trust instantly.

Preventing quiet erosion requires attention to behavior beyond accuracy. Stability, transparency about changes, and consistent communication matter. When systems evolve, users should understand why. When outputs vary, boundaries should remain clear.

Trust is not maintained through persuasion. It is maintained through steadiness. AI systems that recognize this treat reliability as an ongoing responsibility rather than a one-time achievement.

In real work, trust does not disappear overnight. It fades through small signals that accumulate unnoticed. Recognizing these signals early allows organizations to respond before confidence declines too far. Because in AI, as in any system, it is easier to preserve trust than to rebuild it.

Designing AI for Trust

Trust is not an afterthought in AI systems. It is not something added once performance reaches a certain level. Trust is designed from the beginning. Systems either earn it through clarity and predictability, or they struggle to recover from its absence later.

Predictability is the foundation. Users must develop a reliable sense of how the system behaves. This does not mean outputs are always identical. It means behavior stays within understood boundaries. When people can anticipate how the system will respond in familiar situations, confidence grows. When behavior shifts without warning, hesitation replaces reliance.

Clear boundaries are equally important. AI systems should make their scope explicit. What decisions are they meant to support?

Under what conditions should they not be used? When boundaries are visible, users can place the system appropriately within their judgment. Without boundaries, intelligence feels overextended, and overextension invites doubt.

Honest limitations strengthen trust rather than weaken it. Systems that acknowledge uncertainty allow users to calibrate their reliance. If AI presents itself as authoritative in all contexts, any failure feels like betrayal. When it communicates that outputs are suggestions or probabilistic assessments, errors are absorbed more easily. Transparency about limits signals maturity.

Consistency over time reinforces these design choices. Trust is built through repeated interaction. Small, steady contributions matter more than occasional brilliance. Systems that prioritize stable behavior over dramatic capability create space for trust to accumulate gradually.

Designing for trust also requires respecting human judgment. AI systems should complement rather than override responsibility. When people retain agency, they engage more openly. They learn when to rely on intelligence and when to question it. This interaction builds familiarity, which deepens trust.

Change must be handled carefully. AI systems evolve, but evolution should be visible and measured. Sudden shifts in behavior undermine confidence, even if performance improves. Communicating adjustments and preserving core expectations maintain stability.

Trust cannot be engineered through persuasion or branding. It emerges from experience. Design choices that emphasize predictability, clear purpose, and honest communication make that experience reliable.

In real work, AI systems succeed when they feel dependable rather than impressive. Trust grows quietly when intelligence supports decisions without overstating its authority. Designing for trust means prioritizing steadiness over spectacle and clarity over ambition. Over time, these choices allow AI to become part of everyday judgment rather than an uncertain experiment.

When Trust Is Forced, It Breaks

Organizations sometimes attempt to accelerate AI adoption by mandating its use. Policies are issued. Processes are rewritten. Teams are told that certain decisions must now pass through the system. On paper, this approach appears efficient. In practice, forced trust often produces the opposite of what was intended.

Trust cannot be mandated. It is built through experience and understanding. When people are required to rely on a system they do not yet understand or believe in, compliance replaces confidence. They follow the rule, but they do not internalize the judgment behind it.

Compliance creates fragile behavior. Users may accept outputs without engaging critically, simply to satisfy process requirements. This leads to over-reliance in some cases and silent workarounds in others. Some teams will follow the system mechanically, even when context suggests caution. Others will consult it only formally, while continuing to make decisions independently.

Neither outcome builds healthy adoption. In the first case, AI becomes a shield for responsibility. "The system recommended it" becomes a substitute for judgment. In the second, AI becomes symbolic—present in documentation but absent in real decision-making. Both patterns undermine the purpose of introducing intelligence.

Forced trust also increases resistance. When AI is framed as an obligation rather than a support, skepticism hardens. Users feel their expertise is being replaced or diminished. Instead of learning how to collaborate with the system, they look for its weaknesses. Early failures confirm their doubts rather than refine their expectations.

The distinction between compliance and confidence is critical. Compliance ensures usage. Confidence ensures meaningful use. A system can achieve high adoption rates on paper while remaining untrusted in practice. True trust is visible not in frequency of use, but in how naturally intelligence is integrated into judgment.

Mandating AI without preparing for uncertainty also creates risk. If users are not comfortable questioning outputs, mistakes may propagate more easily. Fear of deviating from mandated processes discourages critical thinking. The system becomes authoritative by policy rather than by credibility.

Healthy trust develops when people feel agency. They must be allowed to test, question, and override. This process may feel slower, but it produces durable reliance. Over time, confidence replaces compliance, and AI becomes a tool rather than an imposition.

When trust is forced, it breaks quietly. It surfaces as resistance, passive adoption, or blind dependence. Designing for voluntary confidence, rather than mandatory use, is what allows AI systems to support decisions responsibly. Trust cannot be commanded. It must be earned through steady experience and respectful integration into human work.

What Trust Looks Like in Mature AI Systems

In mature AI systems, trust is visible not in promotional claims, but in everyday behavior. It shows up quietly in how people use the system, how they talk about it, and how naturally it fits into decision-making.

One clear sign of trust is habitual consultation. Users check the system without being reminded. It becomes part of their workflow in the same way other essential tools do. There is no ceremony around its use. It is neither feared nor celebrated. It is simply relied upon.

Trusted systems also invite balanced judgment. People neither follow outputs blindly nor ignore them reflexively. They understand when the system is helpful and when context requires caution. This calibrated use is a strong indicator of maturity. Trust here is not blind confidence. It is informed reliance.

Another pattern is reduced friction. Discussions about the system shift from whether it should be used to how it can be improved. Questions become constructive rather than skeptical. Teams focus on refining integration rather than debating legitimacy. The presence of the system no longer feels experimental.

In mature environments, trust also survives occasional mistakes. When errors occur, they are treated as part of learning rather than proof of failure. Users do not abandon the system after one unexpected outcome. They evaluate what happened and continue using it appropriately. This resilience reflects confidence built over time.

Language changes as well. Instead of referring to "the AI recommendation" as something external, people speak about it as part of their reasoning process. Intelligence becomes embedded in judgment. The system is seen as support, not as an authority to be challenged or obeyed.

Importantly, trusted AI systems do not dominate decisions. They operate within clear boundaries. Users know what the system is responsible for and what remains human. This clarity reduces anxiety and makes reliance comfortable.

Mature trust is steady. It does not depend on constant validation or reassurance. It grows from repeated, consistent experience. AI systems that reach this stage are not described as impressive. They are described as dependable.

In real work, that is what trust looks like: quiet integration, informed reliance, and sustained use. Performance may attract attention, but mature trust is what allows intelligence to endure.

Trust Cannot Be Optimized

In AI work, there is a temptation to treat trust as another variable to improve. If performance increases, trust will follow. If adoption metrics rise, confidence must be growing. This way of thinking misunderstands what trust is and how it forms.

Trust is not a feature that can be engineered directly. It cannot be optimized through messaging or mandates. It grows from repeated interaction under real conditions. People learn to rely on AI systems the same way they learn to rely on colleagues: through steady experience, predictable behavior, and visible responsibility.

Attempts to accelerate trust often backfire. Overstating capability raises expectations beyond what uncertainty allows. Forcing usage creates compliance without confidence. Designing for persuasion rather than clarity produces fragile reliance. Trust built on pressure is easily broken.

Instead, trust accumulates gradually. It strengthens when systems behave consistently, when boundaries are clear, and when limitations are acknowledged openly. It deepens when users are allowed to question and override without penalty. These patterns create familiarity. Familiarity reduces hesitation.

Trust also depends on context. It grows within specific decisions and environments, not universally. Organizations that recognize this allow confidence to develop where it is earned rather than expecting it everywhere at once.

Most importantly, trust is sustained through stewardship. AI systems change. Conditions evolve. Maintaining trust requires attention to stability and communication. It requires humility about what intelligence can and cannot do.

Seeing trust as something that cannot be optimized shifts focus. It encourages patience over pressure and clarity over persuasion. AI systems that endure are those that respect this process. They earn their place in real work slowly, through reliability rather than spectacle.

As this chapter closes, the focus moves closer to the interaction itself. The next chapter explores how humans and systems collaborate in practice—how judgment, feedback, and shared responsibility shape daily use. Trust may not be optimized, but it can be honored. And in AI, honoring trust is what allows intelligence to remain useful over time.

Chapter 8
AI and Human Systems

AI Systems Are Socio-Technical

AI systems are often described as technical artifacts—models, pipelines, algorithms, and infrastructure. But in real work, they are never purely technical. They are socio-technical systems. Their behavior, impact, and value emerge from the interaction between intelligence and people.

Unlike traditional software, AI does not operate on fixed logic alone. It produces probabilistic outputs. It adapts to patterns. It changes behavior as inputs shift. These characteristics mean that AI cannot be fully understood by examining its structure in isolation. Its real meaning appears only when it meets human judgment.

Probabilistic outputs require interpretation. An AI system rarely says "this is correct." It says, in effect, "this is likely." That likelihood must be evaluated by someone. The final decision often remains human, even when the system's influence is strong. In this sense, AI always participates in a broader decision process rather than replacing it entirely.

Learning behavior further connects AI to its environment. As systems adapt based on feedback, they reflect not only data but also human responses. If users ignore certain outputs, override others, or change how they act, the system's evolution may shift accordingly. Intelligence becomes shaped by interaction. It is influenced by how people use it, not just how it was designed.

Organizational context amplifies this dynamic. The same AI system can behave differently in two departments simply because expectations, risk tolerance, and incentives differ. Trust levels vary. Decision authority shifts. What is accepted in one setting may be questioned in another. These human factors alter how intelligence is perceived and applied.

Human judgment also defines boundaries. People decide when to defer to the system and when to intervene. They determine how much uncertainty is acceptable. They choose how errors are handled. These choices shape outcomes as much as the system's internal behavior.

Treating AI as purely technical overlooks this complexity. It leads to designs that optimize performance without considering integration. When adoption struggles, the system is blamed or adjusted technically, even though the challenge may lie in human alignment.

Recognizing AI as socio-technical changes the conversation. It shifts focus from improving models to understanding interaction. It highlights that success depends on clarity of roles, shared responsibility, and cultural readiness.

In real work, AI systems do not act alone. They participate in networks of people, processes, and decisions. Their behavior is co-created. Understanding this relationship is essential for building intelligence that endures. AI cannot be separated from human context because it is shaped by it, influenced by it, and ultimately judged within it.

Humans Shape AI Behavior

AI systems are often described as if they operate independently once deployed. In reality, their behavior is deeply shaped by human interaction. The way people respond to outputs, provide corrections, and choose when to rely on intelligence creates feedback loops that influence how systems evolve over time.

Every AI system exists within a pattern of use. Some outputs are acted upon immediately. Others are questioned, modified, or ignored. These choices are not neutral. They signal what is acceptable, useful, or problematic. Over time, this pattern of responses influences how the system is perceived and, in many cases, how it adapts.

Consider overrides. When users frequently override certain recommendations, they communicate that the system's judgment does not align with context. If this pattern is recognized and incorporated into future adjustments, the system becomes more aligned with real-world needs. If it is ignored, the gap between system behavior and human judgment widens.

Corrections function similarly. When users adjust outputs or provide feedback, they shape the boundaries of acceptable behavior. AI systems that incorporate feedback gradually reflect the preferences and norms of their environment. In this sense, intelligence is not static. It absorbs aspects of organizational culture through repeated interaction.

Usage patterns also matter. If a system is consulted only in specific situations, it becomes specialized around those contexts. If it is relied upon broadly, its influence expands. Patterns of dependence and avoidance both affect how the system integrates into daily work.

Feedback loops can be subtle. Sometimes influence is direct, through explicit corrections. Other times it is indirect, through behavioral signals. Reduced usage may indicate declining trust. Increased reliance may reinforce confidence. These signals shape future decisions about how the system is maintained or adjusted.

Adaptation is not automatic or neutral. It depends on what feedback is captured and how it is interpreted. Human judgment determines which signals matter. In this way, AI systems evolve alongside their users. They are co-shaped by technical behavior and human response.

This dynamic creates responsibility. If human interaction influences AI behavior, then oversight and engagement become essential. Ignoring feedback patterns allows drift. Attending to them enables alignment. Organizations that recognize this relationship treat AI as part of an ongoing conversation rather than a finished product.

Understanding that humans shape AI behavior reframes accountability. It highlights that intelligence is embedded in a loop of action and reaction. Systems improve not only because of technical refinement, but because people interact with them thoughtfully.

In real work, AI does not act in isolation. Its behavior is the result of continuous interaction between human judgment and probabilistic output. Recognizing and managing this feedback loop is central to building intelligence that remains aligned with decisions over time.

When AI Changes How People Work

Introducing an AI system does more than add a new tool. It changes how people think about their work. Even when the system is designed to "assist," it subtly reshapes roles, responsibilities, and decision patterns. These shifts often occur gradually, without formal announcements or structural changes.

AI-specific characteristics drive this transformation. Because outputs are probabilistic, people must interpret them. This interpretation becomes part of the role. A task that once involved making a direct judgment now involves evaluating a recommendation first. The cognitive sequence changes. Instead of asking, "What should I decide?" people begin asking, "Do I agree with the system?"

Over time, this pattern influences expertise. Some individuals become skilled at calibrating AI outputs—knowing when to trust and when to question. Others may defer too quickly or resist unnecessarily. The presence of AI creates a new layer of judgment: judgment about the system itself.

Responsibility also shifts. When decisions are influenced by AI, accountability becomes shared, even if formally unchanged. People may feel more cautious because they are now responsible for overseeing intelligence, not just making choices. In some cases, they may feel less ownership, assuming the system carries part of the burden. Both reactions alter behavior.

AI can also change pacing. Decisions that once required deliberation may accelerate when recommendations are readily available. Alternatively, new verification steps may slow processes as people double-check outputs. The rhythm of work adjusts to accommodate intelligence.

Patterns of collaboration evolve as well. Discussions begin to reference system outputs. Meetings include consideration of what the AI suggested. Over time, intelligence becomes part of collective reasoning. This integration can improve clarity, but it can also narrow focus if outputs are treated as definitive.

Importantly, these changes are rarely dramatic. They accumulate quietly. A role described as "analyst" may gradually become "analyst and AI evaluator." A manager's responsibility may shift from direct decision-making to overseeing how AI informs those decisions. These evolutions are subtle but significant.

AI systems also influence learning. New employees may learn to rely on intelligence earlier in their development. Experienced professionals may adapt by refining how they use recommendations. In both cases, the system becomes part of how expertise is formed.

Recognizing that AI changes how people work encourages deliberate design. It highlights the need to consider not only what the system does, but how it reshapes judgment and responsibility. Ignoring these effects can create confusion about roles and expectations.

In real work, AI is not an addition that leaves everything else untouched. It is an influence that reconfigures decision patterns. Understanding this influence allows organizations to guide change thoughtfully rather than allowing it to emerge unintentionally.

Humans Adapt Faster Than Systems

AI systems are often described as adaptive because they learn from data and evolve over time. Yet in practice, humans adapt faster than the systems they use. When AI is introduced into real work, people begin adjusting immediately. They test boundaries, develop shortcuts, and sometimes create quiet workarounds long before the system itself changes.

This human adaptability is not malicious. It is pragmatic. People are motivated to accomplish tasks efficiently and protect responsibility. If an AI system slows them down, produces outputs that require interpretation, or introduces uncertainty, they respond. They reshape their behavior to reduce friction.

Workarounds are one common pattern. Users may consult the AI only in certain cases, even if it was intended for broader use. They may ignore outputs that do not align with intuition. In some cases, they may prepare inputs differently to produce more predictable results. These adjustments happen quickly because they are under direct human control.

Shortcuts emerge for similar reasons. If interacting with the system feels cumbersome, users streamline the process. They develop informal rules for when to rely on it and when to bypass it. Over time, these shortcuts become habits. The system remains technically unchanged, but its role in practice has shifted.

Silent resistance can also develop. When trust is incomplete, people comply outwardly while limiting reliance. They may document that they consulted the system without meaningfully incorporating its output. This resistance is rarely declared openly. It is visible only in patterns of use.

AI-specific uncertainty accelerates this dynamic. Because outputs are probabilistic, users quickly learn where recommendations feel reliable and where they do not. They adapt behavior accordingly. These adjustments often occur faster than any formal retraining or system update.

The system may continue to evolve gradually through feedback mechanisms, but its pace is structured and deliberate. Human adaptation, by contrast, is immediate. It reflects lived experience rather than planned improvement.

This imbalance has implications. If organizations focus only on refining the system while ignoring how people are adjusting around it, misalignment grows. Architecture may remain unchanged while actual usage diverges from design intent.

Recognizing that humans adapt faster than systems invites closer observation of behavior. It encourages teams to pay attention to patterns of use, not just system outputs. Workarounds and shortcuts are signals. They indicate where integration may be misaligned or expectations unclear.

In real work, AI does not dictate behavior unilaterally. It enters an environment where people are constantly adjusting. Understanding this human responsiveness is essential for maintaining alignment between intention and practice. Systems may be adaptive, but human adaptation is immediate—and it shapes outcomes just as strongly.

Feedback Is Not Optional in AI

AI systems do not remain useful by default. Unlike static tools that perform the same function repeatedly, AI operates within changing environments. Inputs shift. Context evolves. Human expectations adjust. Without continuous feedback, intelligence drifts. In this sense, feedback is not an enhancement. It is a requirement.

AI systems depend on signals from real use. These signals indicate whether outputs are helpful, misaligned, or potentially harmful. When users correct recommendations, override decisions, or question results, they provide information about how the system fits into reality. This information keeps intelligence anchored to purpose.

When feedback is missing, drift begins quietly. A system may continue producing outputs that appear reasonable but no longer match current conditions. Because AI often behaves probabilistically, subtle shifts may not trigger obvious alarms. Over time, alignment erodes. Decisions influenced by the system become less effective, even though performance metrics may not show dramatic change.

Distorted feedback is equally dangerous. If only certain types of signals are captured—perhaps only positive confirmations—the system develops a skewed understanding of its impact. It may reinforce patterns that are convenient rather than correct. In environments where users hesitate to challenge outputs, intelligence can become insulated from reality.

Human behavior shapes feedback quality. If people feel pressured to accept AI recommendations, they may suppress disagreement. If overrides are discouraged, corrective signals disappear. The system then adapts based on incomplete information. In such cases, feedback loops amplify misalignment rather than reduce it.

Feedback also supports safety. AI systems influence decisions that may carry risk. Continuous observation and correction help identify emerging problems before they escalate. Without structured attention to feedback, issues surface only after consequences become visible.

Importantly, feedback is not limited to explicit corrections. Patterns of use provide signals as well. Reduced reliance may indicate declining trust. Increased consultation may reflect growing confidence. Interpreting these behavioral cues is part of maintaining alignment.

Treating feedback as optional creates the illusion of stability. The system appears to function independently, but its relevance gradually weakens. Organizations may assume that intelligence, once deployed, will sustain itself. This assumption overlooks the dynamic nature of real work.

Mature AI use recognizes feedback as an ongoing responsibility. It acknowledges that intelligence must be monitored and recalibrated. This is not a sign of weakness in the system. It is a reflection of how environments change.

In real work, AI systems remain useful and safe only when human judgment remains engaged. Feedback is the mechanism through which that engagement shapes behavior. Without it, intelligence becomes detached from context. With it, AI can continue to support decisions responsibly over time.

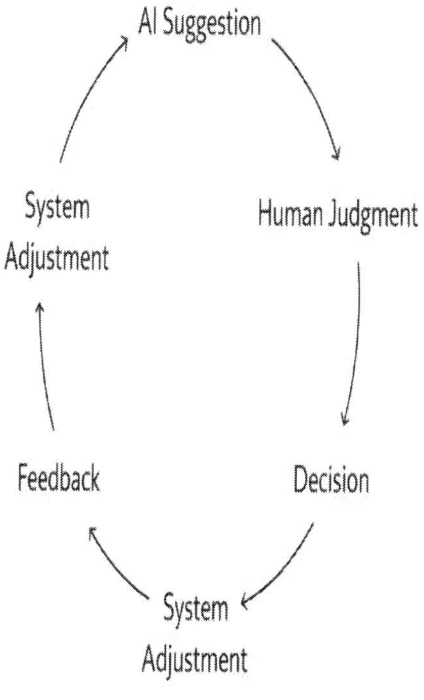

Figure 6. The Human–AI Interaction Loop

Responsibility Does Not Disappear

When AI systems begin influencing decisions, a subtle psychological shift can occur. Because intelligence is involved, it can feel as though responsibility is shared—or even transferred. Recommendations carry an air of objectivity. Outputs appear calculated rather than chosen. Yet regardless of how advanced a system becomes, responsibility does not disappear. It remains human.

AI systems generate probabilistic outputs. They suggest, rank, estimate, or classify. They do not carry consequences. People do. When a decision leads to financial loss, reputational damage, operational disruption, or even physical harm, it is individuals and organizations that answer for it. The presence of AI does not change that structure of accountability.

This becomes especially visible in high-consequence environments. In defense and wireless security contexts, AI systems may detect anomalous signals, flag potential intrusions, or classify patterns as suspicious. The system can estimate likelihood. It can prioritize alerts. It can even simulate possible scenarios. But the decision to escalate, isolate a network, initiate countermeasures, or ignore a signal remains human. If the response is excessive, resources are wasted. If it is insufficient, exposure increases. The system informs. The human answers.

This gap between influence and responsibility creates risk. If a system's output is treated as authoritative, decision-makers may feel shielded. "The system recommended it" becomes an explanation rather than a justification. Over time, this mindset weakens judgment. Accountability becomes blurred because responsibility feels diffused.

AI-specific responsibility gaps often appear at handoff points. A system produces an output. A human reviews it. An action is taken. When outcomes are questioned, it becomes unclear whether the issue lies in the model's behavior, the human's interpretation, or the organizational process around it. Without clarity, accountability becomes difficult to trace.

Another gap emerges when AI systems evolve. Learning behavior means outputs may shift over time. In dynamic environments such as cybersecurity or defense modeling, adaptation can subtly change how threats are ranked or classified. If adjustments occur without explicit oversight, decisions may change without anyone consciously approving that shift. Responsibility must include monitoring adaptation, not just initial deployment.

There is also the risk of over-reliance. When AI consistently performs well, confidence grows. This is natural. But when confidence turns into unquestioned acceptance, responsibility quietly erodes. Decision-makers may stop critically evaluating outputs. In high-stakes systems, that erosion is dangerous because errors propagate faster than hesitation.

Maintaining responsibility requires explicit design. Roles must be clear. Who reviews outputs? Who can override them? Who monitors long-term behavior? Who validates that adaptation aligns with intent? These questions are not technical; they are organizational. Without answers, intelligence operates in a space where influence exceeds accountability.

Recognizing that responsibility does not disappear encourages humility. AI systems can inform, accelerate, and improve decisions. They cannot bear consequences. Human oversight remains essential, not because systems are flawed, but because decisions affect people, infrastructure, and institutions.

In mature AI use, accountability is visible. It is not hidden behind performance metrics or system outputs. People understand that intelligence is a tool within a larger decision process. This clarity protects both trust and integrity.

As AI becomes more integrated into real work, the temptation to treat it as autonomous will grow. Resisting that temptation is critical. Responsibility cannot be automated. It can only be exercised. And in the presence of intelligence, it becomes even more important to keep it clearly human.

Designing for Human Behavior

AI systems are often designed with ideal users in mind. The assumption is that people will read every output carefully, interpret uncertainty rationally, and apply judgment consistently. In real work, this assumption rarely holds. Human attention is limited. Incentives are uneven. Judgment is shaped by pressure and context. Designing AI without accounting for these realities creates friction.

Attention is the first constraint. People do not have unlimited time to evaluate recommendations. They operate under deadlines and competing priorities. If an AI system requires extensive interpretation, it will be used selectively or ignored. Designing for human behavior means presenting intelligence in a way that respects cognitive limits. Outputs must be clear enough to support quick understanding without demanding constant scrutiny.

Incentives also shape behavior. Individuals respond to how they are evaluated and rewarded. If performance metrics prioritize speed over accuracy, users may rely on AI differently than intended. If accountability is strict, they may hesitate to act on recommendations. AI systems cannot be separated from these incentive structures. Ignoring them leads to misalignment between design intent and actual use.

Judgment varies by experience and role. A senior decision-maker may interpret uncertainty differently than a new team member. If AI systems assume uniform expertise, confusion follows. Designing for human behavior means acknowledging variability. It requires clarity about when the system should guide strongly and when it should defer.

There is also the reality of fatigue. Over time, repeated exposure to recommendations can create either over-reliance or disengagement. If outputs are too frequent, they become background noise. If they are too sparse, users forget the system's presence. Balancing visibility with restraint is part of designing for sustained use.

Human behavior includes resistance as well. When people feel their expertise is undermined, they may push back quietly. If AI is positioned as a replacement rather than support, adoption slows. Systems designed with respect for human contribution foster cooperation instead of defensiveness.

Designing for human behavior also means expecting error. People will misinterpret outputs. They will sometimes override correctly and sometimes incorrectly. AI systems must accommodate these variations without amplifying them. Clarity about roles and boundaries helps maintain stability.

Ultimately, AI systems succeed when they align with how people actually work, not how designers hope they will. This alignment requires observation and adjustment. It recognizes that intelligence operates within human limits, not above them.

In real work, thoughtful design respects attention, incentives, and judgment. It anticipates variability rather than resisting it. AI that fits naturally into human behavior earns steady adoption. AI that assumes ideal behavior creates friction. Designing with realism is what allows intelligence to support decisions without distorting them.

When Humans Become the Bottleneck

AI systems are often introduced with the promise of removing bottlenecks. By automating analysis or generating recommendations quickly, they appear to accelerate decision-making. In practice, however, intelligence can expose a different constraint. As systems become faster and more capable, human capacity for review, interpretation, and accountability may become the limiting factor.

This is not a failure of people. It is a reflection of how decision processes work. AI can generate more insights than humans can comfortably absorb. When outputs increase, so does the burden of evaluation. Each recommendation requires attention. Each signal invites judgment. Over time, this accumulation can create decision overload.

Review fatigue is a common outcome. When users must evaluate many AI-generated suggestions, their ability to engage thoughtfully declines. They may begin approving recommendations quickly to keep pace. Alternatively, they may delay action because the volume feels overwhelming. In both cases, the bottleneck shifts from analysis to attention.

Hesitation can also increase. As AI systems surface more possibilities, decision-makers may feel greater pressure to consider each one carefully. The presence of intelligence raises expectations of precision. People may worry about overlooking an important signal. This caution slows processes that were once simpler.

AI-specific uncertainty amplifies these effects. Because outputs are probabilistic rather than definitive, each requires interpretation. The responsibility to weigh likelihoods and context remains human. If the system generates more recommendations than can be realistically assessed, the bottleneck is not technical. It is cognitive.

In some environments, organizations respond by adding layers of oversight. Additional reviewers are introduced. More approvals are required. While intended to manage risk, these measures can compound delay. The system produces intelligence quickly, but human processes cannot absorb it efficiently.

Recognizing humans as the bottleneck invites a different response. Rather than attempting to replace judgment entirely, mature systems respect its limits. They prioritize relevance over volume. They surface fewer, clearer signals aligned with defined decisions.

When AI highlights human constraints, it provides insight. It reveals where processes are overloaded or where responsibility is unclear. This visibility can prompt refinement. It can encourage organizations to simplify decision paths rather than accelerate output indiscriminately.

Seeing humans as a bottleneck should not be framed as criticism. It is an acknowledgment of reality. Human judgment carries accountability and context. AI may increase speed, but people remain responsible for consequences.

Balanced AI design aligns system output with human capacity. It ensures intelligence supports decisions without overwhelming those who must make them. In real work, acceleration without absorption creates friction. Respecting human limits allows AI to enhance rather than strain the decision process.

What Mature Human–AI Interaction Looks Like

In mature environments, human–AI interaction is rarely dramatic. It does not feel like a constant negotiation between machine and judgment. Instead, it settles into a rhythm. The system supports decisions quietly, and people understand how to work alongside it without friction.

Trust is visible in how naturally the AI is consulted. Users do not approach it with suspicion, nor do they rely on it blindly. They understand its role. When facing a relevant decision, they include its input as part of their reasoning process. The interaction feels integrated rather than imposed.

Rhythm is another sign of maturity. The system surfaces intelligence at moments that align with real work. It does not interrupt unnecessarily, and it does not remain silent when support is needed. Over time, this timing becomes predictable. People know when to expect guidance and when to proceed independently. This predictability reduces cognitive strain.

Shared responsibility defines the relationship. AI systems contribute analysis and perspective, but humans retain ownership of outcomes. When recommendations are followed, people stand behind them. When they are overridden, the reasoning is intentional rather than reactive. There is clarity about where judgment resides.

In mature interaction, uncertainty is acknowledged openly. AI outputs are treated as informed suggestions rather than directives. Users feel comfortable questioning them. The system's limitations are understood, and this understanding reduces tension. Mistakes are addressed through reflection rather than blame.

Language changes as well. Instead of saying "the system decided," teams say "we decided, informed by the system." This subtle shift signals ownership. AI becomes part of collective reasoning rather than a separate authority.

Importantly, mature interaction reduces noise. There are fewer unnecessary alerts and fewer ambiguous signals. Intelligence is aligned with specific decisions. The system's presence feels purposeful rather than overwhelming.

This balance does not emerge automatically. It develops through consistent use, feedback, and refinement. Over time, collaboration between human judgment and AI becomes routine.

In real work, mature human–AI interaction is steady. It is defined by trust that has been earned, a rhythm that fits daily processes, and responsibility that remains visible. Intelligence becomes a partner in decision-making, not a substitute for it.

AI Never Works Alone

AI systems are often described as if they operate independently—analyzed, deployed, and left to perform. In reality, AI never works alone. It functions within human systems shaped by judgment, incentives, habits, and responsibility. Every output enters a chain of interpretation. Every recommendation is filtered through context.

Even the most advanced intelligence relies on people to define its purpose. Humans decide which problems matter, which decisions should be influenced, and which risks are acceptable. These choices shape the boundaries within which AI operates. Without them, intelligence has no direction.

AI also depends on human attention. Outputs must be reviewed, interpreted, and acted upon. Feedback must be observed and incorporated. When people disengage, the system's relevance fades. When they engage thoughtfully, intelligence becomes aligned with real needs.

Responsibility anchors this relationship. Decisions influenced by AI still carry consequences for individuals and organizations. Accountability does not migrate into the system. It remains human. This fact ensures that AI cannot function in isolation. It participates in decisions but does not own them.

Over time, AI becomes woven into routines. It shapes how work is performed and how judgment is exercised. Yet even at this stage, it remains part of a broader socio-technical environment. Trust, oversight, and context continue to influence outcomes.

Recognizing that AI never works alone changes expectations. It reduces the temptation to treat intelligence as autonomous or self-sufficient. It encourages attention to the human structures around the system: roles, communication, and responsibility.

As AI adoption expands, this awareness becomes more important. Scaling intelligence without strengthening the human systems around it increases risk. Growth magnifies both strengths and weaknesses. The quality of interaction determines whether scaling produces value or instability.

The next chapter turns toward this challenge. It explores how organizations extend AI responsibly, preserving trust and clarity as systems influence more decisions. Intelligence may operate quickly and adaptively, but it always does so within human frameworks.

AI never works alone. And understanding that relationship is what allows it to remain useful as it grows.

Chapter 9
Scaling Without Losing Control

Scaling Changes AI Behavior

AI systems rarely behave the same way at scale as they do in small, controlled deployments. In early stages, usage is limited. Context is narrow. Feedback is direct. As systems expand across teams, departments, or geographies, the environment changes—and so does the behavior of the system.

At small scale, feedback loops are relatively simple. A limited group of users interacts with the system. Corrections are visible. Misalignment is easier to detect. Adaptation, when it occurs, reflects a relatively consistent set of expectations. In these conditions, behavior feels stable.

I have seen this clearly in financial services environments. A credit risk model that performs consistently within one regional lending team can appear highly reliable. The customer profile is relatively uniform. Regulatory expectations are consistent. Risk appetite is aligned. But when the same model is deployed across multiple countries or business units, differences begin to surface. Local risk tolerances vary. Economic conditions differ. Operational workflows are not identical. The model has not changed—but the environment has. And its behavior, in practice, begins to look different.

When AI scales, feedback becomes more complex. Different users bring different interpretations, risk tolerances, and usage patterns. Some may rely heavily on outputs. Others may override frequently. These varied interactions send mixed signals into the system. Over time, adaptation reflects not a single environment, but many. Behavior may become less predictable because it is responding to a broader and sometimes conflicting set of inputs.

Data drift becomes more pronounced at scale. As AI systems influence decisions across larger populations, they begin to shape the very data they receive. Recommendations affect behavior, and behavior changes future inputs. In small deployments, this loop may be limited. At scale, the effect compounds. Subtle shifts in context can alter outcomes in ways that were not visible earlier.

Interaction effects also emerge. Decisions influenced by AI in one part of the organization may affect conditions in another. What appears as an isolated improvement locally may create unintended consequences elsewhere. These cross-effects rarely surface in pilot environments. They become visible only when systems operate broadly.

Scaling also increases exposure to edge cases. In small groups, unusual situations may be rare. At larger scale, rare events become frequent simply because the population grows. AI systems must handle greater variability. Behavior that seemed stable in limited settings may appear inconsistent under broader conditions.

Trust dynamics change as well. At small scale, relationships between users and systems are personal. At scale, trust becomes distributed. Perception varies across teams. A single failure can propagate widely, affecting confidence beyond the original context.

Importantly, scaling does not merely increase volume. It alters the environment in which intelligence operates. Feedback loops become layered. Adaptation interacts with diverse usage patterns. The system begins to participate in a network of influences rather than a contained workflow.

Recognizing that scaling changes AI behavior encourages caution. Systems that perform well locally should not be assumed to behave identically when expanded. Scaling requires renewed attention to boundaries, feedback, and responsibility.

In real work, growth magnifies both strengths and weaknesses. AI systems that are stable at small scale must be re-examined as they expand. Because at scale, intelligence does not just operate more—it operates differently.

What Works for One Team Breaks at Scale

An AI system that performs well within a single team often appears ready for broader adoption. The use case is clear. The decision path is understood. Feedback is direct. Success feels transferable. Yet when the same system is expanded across teams, regions, or new contexts, performance and trust often shift. What worked locally begins to strain.

One reason is variability. A single team typically shares norms, language, and expectations. They interpret outputs similarly. They operate within the same risk tolerance and workflow rhythm. AI systems tuned within this environment reflect those shared assumptions. When expanded, those assumptions no longer hold.

I have seen this in highly technical environments as well. A predictive model developed to support yield optimization in a semiconductor research setting worked effectively within one group of engineers. The data interpretation standards were aligned.

The domain vocabulary was shared. The tolerance for experimentation was understood. But when similar logic was introduced to adjacent teams working under different production pressures, expectations shifted. Some teams prioritized experimental exploration. Others required strict reproducibility. The same system began to feel "unreliable" to one group and "too rigid" to another—not because it changed, but because context did.

Different teams make decisions differently. Some prioritize speed. Others prioritize caution. Some treat AI outputs as advisory. Others expect stronger direction. The same recommendation may be acted upon confidently in one group and questioned in another. This diversity of judgment alters how the system's outputs are experienced.

Context loss is another factor. In small deployments, designers often work closely with users. Nuances are understood. Edge cases are discussed openly. When scaling occurs, that proximity disappears. New users inherit a system shaped by decisions they were not part of. The rationale behind boundaries or limitations may not be visible. Without context, trust weakens.

Regional and cultural differences amplify this effect. Interpretations of risk, authority, and responsibility vary across locations. An AI system embedded in one cultural environment may feel misaligned in another. Even when outputs are technically consistent, expectations differ.

Decision diversity also increases at scale. A system designed to support a specific decision may gradually be applied to adjacent ones. Users stretch its purpose because it appears capable. This expansion introduces scenarios the original design did not anticipate. Performance may degrade, not because the system failed, but because it was repurposed without recalibration.

Feedback loops change as well. In a single team, corrective signals are coherent. At scale, feedback becomes fragmented. Conflicting adjustments may push the system in competing directions. Behavior becomes less stable because alignment is less unified.

Scaling also exposes governance challenges. Who owns adjustments? Who defines acceptable risk? Without clarity, expansion magnifies uncertainty.

Recognizing that what works for one team may break at scale encourages humility. Success in a controlled environment does not guarantee universal fit. Expansion requires revisiting assumptions about context, decision types, and boundaries.

In real work, AI systems are shaped by the environments they inhabit. When that environment expands, behavior changes. Scaling is not replication. It is transformation. Treating it as such allows organizations to adapt thoughtfully rather than assuming continuity where it may not exist.

Trust Does Not Scale Automatically

When an AI system earns trust within a small group, it is tempting to assume that confidence will expand naturally with it. If one team relies on the system comfortably, why wouldn't others? In practice, trust does not scale automatically. It must be rebuilt, reinforced, and sometimes re-earned as the system reaches new contexts.

Trust is shaped by experience. In early deployments, users develop familiarity through repeated interaction. They learn where the system performs well and where it requires caution. They form calibrated expectations. When the system expands to new teams or regions, that experiential foundation does not transfer. New users encounter the system without shared history. They begin again at the stage of cautious evaluation.

Scaling also introduces inconsistency. AI systems that operate across diverse contexts may behave differently because inputs vary. Edge cases become more common. Situations that were rare in a pilot setting may surface regularly at scale. These variations can create the perception that the system is unstable, even if its underlying behavior remains technically sound.

Expectation mismatch compounds this challenge. In smaller settings, expectations are often shaped through close communication between designers and users. As the system scales, messaging becomes broader and less tailored. Some groups may expect high reliability. Others may expect advisory support. When outputs do not match these varied expectations, confidence weakens.

AI-specific uncertainty intensifies trust erosion. Because outputs are probabilistic, subtle shifts in performance are interpreted differently across contexts. A deviation that is acceptable in one environment may be unacceptable in another. Without clear boundaries and communication, users may generalize isolated experiences into broader doubt.

Trust at scale also depends on governance. Who addresses concerns? Who explains unexpected behavior? In smaller deployments, these roles are visible. At scale, distance grows between users and system stewards. When issues arise, delayed responses can erode confidence quickly.

Importantly, trust does not decline only through major failures. It can fade through small inconsistencies amplified across many users. A minor misunderstanding in one team may become a widespread perception when repeated elsewhere.

Recognizing that trust must be reinforced at scale changes how expansion is approached. It encourages deliberate onboarding, transparent communication, and renewed clarity about boundaries. Scaling is not simply a technical rollout. It is a relational process.

In real work, trust is local before it is global. It grows through lived experience. As AI systems expand, they enter new human environments with different expectations and pressures. Treating trust as something that scales automatically overlooks this reality.

Intelligence may replicate easily. Trust does not. It must be cultivated wherever the system operates. And at scale, that cultivation requires as much attention as the technology itself.

Governance Emerges Whether You Design It or Not

As AI systems expand across teams and decisions, governance does not remain optional. Even if no formal structure is defined, patterns of control and responsibility begin to form. People create informal rules. Workarounds develop. Decisions are shaped by habits rather than design. Governance emerges whether it is intentional or not.

In small deployments, oversight is often implicit. A limited group understands the system. Questions are resolved through conversation. Responsibility is clear because proximity is close. As scaling occurs, that clarity weakens. More users interact with the system. Interpretations vary. Without explicit boundaries, informal norms begin to fill the gap.

AI-specific responsibility gaps accelerate this process. Because outputs are probabilistic and influence decisions indirectly, it is not always obvious who owns outcomes. When a recommendation leads to an unexpected result, users may assume someone else is accountable. In the absence of defined roles, responsibility disperses.

Workarounds often appear first. Teams adjust how they use the system to match their needs. Some may rely on it selectively. Others may build parallel processes to double-check outputs. These adaptations are rational responses to uncertainty. Over time, they become informal governance mechanisms. They shape how AI is actually used, even if they were never formally approved.

Shadow decisions can also arise. When confidence in the system is uneven, individuals may override outputs quietly or reinterpret them without documentation. This behavior is not necessarily defiance. It reflects a need to manage risk locally. However, it creates inconsistency across the organization.

As AI scales, feedback channels may become fragmented. Concerns raised in one area may not reach those responsible for oversight. Adjustments may occur unevenly. Without clear stewardship, the system's evolution reflects scattered inputs rather than coordinated guidance.

Importantly, governance is not only about control. It is about clarity. Who monitors changes in behavior? Who defines acceptable boundaries? Who addresses recurring confusion? If these questions are unanswered, informal answers will emerge through practice.

Allowing governance to form unintentionally can create misalignment. Informal rules may conflict across teams. Responsibility may remain ambiguous. Trust may erode unevenly. Over time, the organization adapts to a system that no one fully oversees.

Recognizing that governance emerges naturally encourages proactive design. It shifts attention from reactive correction to deliberate clarity. AI systems, especially at scale, influence decisions widely. They require visible ownership and coherent guidance.

In real work, governance is not an external constraint. It is a structural response to shared responsibility. When designed thoughtfully, it supports trust and alignment. When left to chance, it forms anyway—often in ways that are inconsistent and difficult to manage.

Scaling Amplifies Misalignment

AI systems are often introduced into environments that are already imperfect. Objectives may be loosely defined. Ownership may be shared ambiguously. Incentives may point in different directions. At small scale, these weaknesses can remain manageable. As AI scales, they do not remain neutral. They are amplified.

AI has a particular tendency to magnify existing patterns. If objectives are unclear, the system learns from signals that reflect that ambiguity. Recommendations may appear inconsistent because the underlying goal was never precise. At limited scale, this may surface as minor confusion. When expanded across teams, the confusion multiplies.

Ownership gaps become more visible as influence grows. In a small deployment, informal agreements may suffice. People know who to ask when something feels wrong. At scale, distance increases. When outputs influence more decisions, responsibility must be explicit. If it is not, errors propagate without clear accountability. What was once a manageable gray area becomes systemic risk.

Incentives also shape AI behavior. If teams are rewarded for speed rather than quality, reliance patterns will reflect that pressure. AI may be used aggressively to accelerate decisions. If risk avoidance dominates incentives, users may override recommendations frequently. At scale, these behaviors accumulate. The system begins to reflect the strongest incentives in the environment, not necessarily the intended purpose.

AI's probabilistic nature intensifies misalignment. Because outputs require interpretation, users apply local judgment. If interpretations differ widely, decision patterns diverge. The same recommendation may lead to different actions in different contexts. At small scale, this variability may be tolerated. At scale, it produces inconsistency that undermines trust.

Feedback loops compound the effect. When AI influences decisions broadly, it shapes the data it later receives. If misaligned objectives drive early behavior, that behavior becomes embedded in future inputs. The system learns from distorted signals, reinforcing the original misalignment.

Scaling also increases visibility. Small inconsistencies that once affected a handful of users now affect many. Perception shifts quickly. A localized issue becomes an organizational concern. Trust declines faster because more people experience the impact simultaneously.

Recognizing that scaling amplifies misalignment encourages deliberate preparation. Before expansion, objectives must be clarified. Ownership must be defined. Incentives must be examined. Scaling does not correct weaknesses. It enlarges them.

In real work, AI systems reflect the environments in which they operate. When aligned conditions exist, scaling spreads value. When misalignment persists, scaling spreads confusion. Intelligence magnifies what is already present. Understanding this dynamic allows organizations to address foundational issues before growth makes them harder to manage.

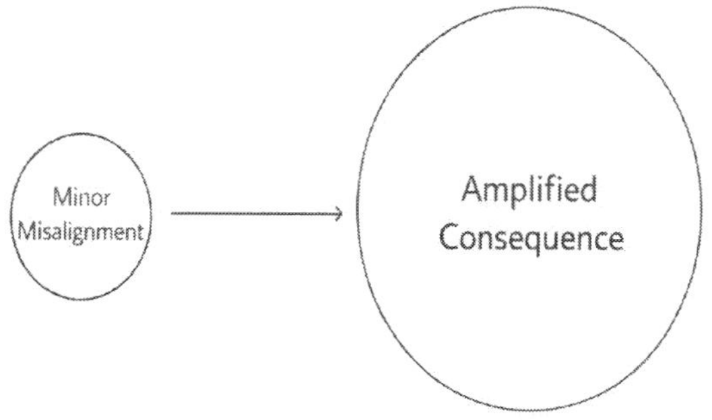

Figure 7. Scale Amplifies Patterns

Centralization vs Local Judgment

As AI systems scale, organizations often face a structural question: should intelligence be centralized or distributed? Centralization promises consistency. A single system influences decisions across teams, reducing duplication and aligning behavior. At the same time, local human judgment remains essential. Tension arises when centralized intelligence meets diverse, context-specific decisions.

Centralized AI systems are attractive because they create uniformity. A common model can standardize recommendations across regions or departments. This consistency reduces fragmentation and can improve fairness. It also simplifies oversight, as responsibility for system behavior is concentrated.

However, AI-specific risks emerge when centralization goes too far. Intelligence trained on aggregated data may overlook local nuance. Patterns that are strong globally may not hold in specific contexts. When a centralized system applies generalized reasoning to localized decisions, misalignment appears.

Probabilistic outputs amplify this tension. AI recommendations reflect statistical tendencies. Local environments often contain exceptions shaped by culture, regulation, or customer behavior. If centralized systems are treated as authoritative, local judgment may be suppressed. Decisions may become consistent but less appropriate.

Over-centralization can also weaken accountability. When intelligence is distant from its users, feedback becomes indirect. Local teams may feel less ownership of outcomes because decisions appear to originate elsewhere. This distance slows adaptation. Signals about misalignment may not reach system stewards quickly.

At the same time, excessive localization introduces its own challenges. If every team modifies or interprets AI outputs independently, coherence erodes. Decision patterns diverge. Trust becomes uneven. The organization may lose the benefits of shared learning.

The tension is not between right and wrong, but between stability and relevance. Centralization supports stability and oversight. Local judgment supports contextual accuracy. Mature AI design balances both.

Clear boundaries help manage this balance. Centralized systems can define core principles and decision frameworks, while allowing space for local interpretation within those limits. Responsibility must remain visible at both levels. Local teams should understand when to defer and when to adapt.

AI systems that respect local judgment often perform better at scale because they acknowledge variability. They treat centralized intelligence as guidance rather than command. This approach preserves coherence without suppressing expertise.

In real work, neither extreme succeeds alone. Centralized AI without local judgment risks rigidity. Local autonomy without shared structure risks fragmentation. The goal is not to eliminate tension, but to manage it thoughtfully.

As AI systems expand, organizations must decide how much authority to centralize and how much judgment to preserve locally. The answer shapes trust, accountability, and effectiveness. Balancing these forces allows intelligence to scale without disconnecting from the human contexts in which decisions are made.

When Scaling Creates New Risk

Scaling an AI system is often seen as a sign of success. If intelligence supports decisions in one team, extending it across the organization appears logical. Yet growth does more than increase reach. It changes the risk profile of the system. What was manageable at small scale can become significant when multiplied.

One of the most immediate risks is error propagation. In a limited deployment, a flawed recommendation affects a small group. At scale, the same error can influence hundreds or thousands of decisions before it is noticed. Because AI systems often operate consistently, mistakes are replicated systematically. This consistency is powerful when correct and costly when misaligned.

Over-reliance is another scaling risk. As AI becomes embedded in daily workflows, users may grow comfortable with its outputs. Confidence, built gradually, can turn into habitual dependence.

When reliance spreads broadly, a single flaw has amplified consequences. The issue is not incompetence, but the natural human tendency to trust tools that have performed well historically.

Scaling also increases exposure to edge cases. Rare scenarios that were negligible in early phases become statistically inevitable in larger populations. AI systems must handle greater variability. Situations outside initial assumptions become frequent enough to matter. If boundaries were loosely defined, these edge cases surface unpredictably.

Feedback loops intensify at scale. AI influences decisions, and those decisions shape future inputs. When systems operate widely, this loop becomes stronger. Small biases or misinterpretations can reinforce themselves over time. Without attentive oversight, the system may drift gradually while appearing stable.

Another risk emerges in responsibility diffusion. As more teams interact with the system, ownership can become unclear. When an outcome is influenced by centralized intelligence but enacted locally, accountability may be ambiguous. This gap complicates response when issues arise.

Scaling also affects perception. A minor inconsistency that might be overlooked in a small setting becomes visible when experienced by many users. Trust can decline rapidly if problems appear widespread, even if the underlying issue is contained.

Importantly, these risks are not arguments against scaling. They are reminders that growth alters dynamics. Systems designed for small environments may require structural reinforcement before expansion.

Recognizing that scaling creates new risk encourages proactive reflection. It prompts organizations to reassess boundaries, oversight, and feedback mechanisms before influence widens. Growth should be accompanied by renewed clarity, not assumptions of continuity.

In real work, scaling multiplies both strengths and weaknesses. AI systems that are stable and well-governed can deliver broader value. Systems with unresolved gaps will see those gaps expand. Understanding this shift allows organizations to grow responsibly rather than reactively.

Designing for Responsible Scale

Scaling AI responsibly is not about accelerating deployment. It is about preserving clarity and trust as influence expands. Growth should feel deliberate rather than abrupt. When intelligence reaches more decisions, the structures around it must grow with equal care.

Gradual expansion is one of the most effective safeguards. AI systems that move step by step allow patterns to stabilize before widening their reach. Each phase of growth provides insight into how behavior changes under new conditions. This pacing protects trust because users can adapt alongside the system.

Clarity must be reinforced at every stage. As new teams adopt the system, its purpose should be restated plainly. What decisions does it support? Where should judgment remain human? Scaling without revisiting these boundaries invites confusion. Responsible growth means repeating and refining the core intent rather than assuming it is understood universally.

Ownership becomes more important as reach increases. Clear stewardship ensures that responsibility does not diffuse. Someone must monitor system behavior, interpret feedback, and address emerging concerns. When users know who stands behind the system, confidence remains steady even as scale increases.

Communication also shapes responsible scale. Changes in behavior, adjustments in scope, or observed limitations should be acknowledged openly. Transparency reduces speculation. It allows trust to extend beyond early adopters to those encountering the system for the first time.

Responsible scale also respects human capacity. Expanding intelligence should not overwhelm decision-makers with excessive output. Systems must remain aligned with how people actually work. Growth that amplifies noise rather than clarity erodes confidence quickly.

Finally, scaling should include reflection. Each expansion phase should prompt questions about alignment and impact. Are decisions improving? Are patterns of use consistent with intent? Responsible scale treats growth as an opportunity to reassess rather than simply extend.

AI systems can scale without losing control when clarity travels with them. Trust does not expand automatically; it follows deliberate design and steady stewardship. Responsible scale is not about doing more faster. It is about growing influence without diluting accountability.

In real work, sustainable growth feels stable. It maintains boundaries, reinforces purpose, and keeps responsibility visible. When AI systems are designed with this mindset, scale becomes an extension of maturity rather than a source of instability.

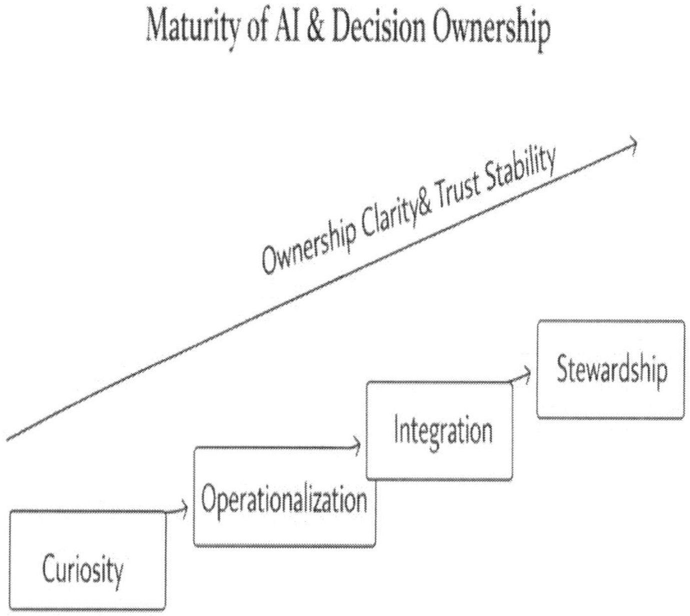

Figure 8. Maturity of AI and Decision Ownership

A Simple Test Before Scaling AI

Before expanding an AI system across teams or decisions, it is worth pausing to ask a simple question: If this system influences twice as many decisions tomorrow, would we understand and own the consequences?

This question brings clarity quickly. Scaling multiplies impact. If the system produces an unexpected result today, can you trace how the decision was made? Can you explain who reviewed it, who approved it, and how feedback will adjust future behavior? If the answer feels uncertain at small scale, expansion will only magnify that uncertainty.

A second question is equally important: Is trust stable, or is it fragile?
Stable trust is quiet and consistent. Users rely on the system appropriately, question it when necessary, and understand its boundaries. Fragile trust, by contrast, depends on recent success or limited exposure. If confidence would collapse after a visible mistake, the system is not ready for broader reach.

These questions are AI-specific because intelligence influences patterns, not just isolated tasks. Scaling does not simply increase usage; it increases influence over decisions. If decision impact is unclear or responsibility feels diffused, growth introduces risk faster than value.

In practice, applying these questions means observing behavior rather than performance claims. Are users acting differently because of the system? Is that change intentional? Do they know when to override recommendations? Can concerns be raised and addressed without confusion?

If decision impact is visible, trust is steady, and responsibility is clearly owned, scaling becomes an extension of maturity. If these elements are uncertain, expansion should pause. Growth without clarity often creates instability that is harder to correct later.

A simple test before scaling is not a barrier to progress. It is a safeguard against unintended amplification. AI systems magnify what they touch. Ensuring that alignment, trust, and ownership are strong at small scale protects outcomes as influence grows.

Scaling is powerful. Asking the right questions beforehand keeps that power constructive rather than disruptive.

Scale Reveals the Truth

At small scale, many weaknesses remain hidden. Assumptions feel stable because they are rarely tested. Trust appears strong because exposure is limited. Objectives seem clear because only a few people interpret them. Early success can create the impression that the system is ready for anything.

Scaling removes that illusion.

When AI systems expand, they encounter diversity—of context, judgment, incentives, and expectations. What was once implicit must now be explicit. What was tolerated quietly becomes visible. Growth does not create new characteristics as much as it exposes existing ones.

If objectives were loosely defined, scaling reveals inconsistency in outcomes. If ownership was informal, expansion exposes responsibility gaps. If trust was built on proximity rather than clarity, distance weakens it quickly. Scaling functions as a stress test. It shows whether alignment was genuine or simply unchallenged.

AI systems, by their nature, amplify patterns. When those patterns are coherent, growth spreads value. When they are fragile, growth spreads instability. Feedback loops become stronger. Small misalignments compound. What seemed manageable in isolation becomes consequential at scale.

Importantly, this revelation is not negative. It is diagnostic. Scaling provides clarity. It highlights where boundaries must be reinforced and where assumptions must be revisited. It offers an opportunity to mature the system rather than retreat from it.

Organizations that understand this treat scale as a moment of reflection, not just expansion. They expect friction. They anticipate adjustment. They see growth not as replication, but as transformation.

As this chapter closes, the perspective shifts from expansion to endurance. Scaling tests structure. The final chapter turns toward longevity—how AI thinking must evolve over time, beyond initial deployment and growth. Because influence that lasts requires more than technical strength. It requires sustained clarity.

Scale reveals the truth. And that truth, when acknowledged, becomes the foundation for long-term intelligence.

Over time, scale also reshapes perception. What once felt innovative becomes routine. What once felt fast begins to feel slow. As more people depend on the system, tolerance for inconsistency declines. Expectations rise. Visibility increases. In this environment, discipline matters more than enthusiasm. Systems that endure are not those that expanded quickly, but those that expanded deliberately.

Chapter 10
The Long-Term Responsibility of AI

AI Is a Long-Term Commitment

AI is often introduced as a project. It has a start date, a budget, a deployment milestone. Once the system is launched, attention shifts elsewhere. This framing is understandable, but it is incomplete. AI is not a one-time implementation. It is an ongoing commitment.

Unlike static systems, AI changes over time. Even when the underlying model remains stable, the environment around it does not. Inputs evolve. User behavior shifts. Business priorities adjust. Because AI systems respond to patterns in data, any change in those patterns affects outcomes. This dynamic nature makes long-term attention essential.

Learning behavior deepens this responsibility. When systems adapt based on feedback, they incorporate the signals they receive. If feedback is consistent and aligned with clear objectives, adaptation strengthens performance. If feedback is uneven or distorted, the system drifts. Drift rarely announces itself loudly. It appears gradually, as subtle changes in recommendations or confidence levels. Without deliberate monitoring, these shifts may go unnoticed until impact becomes visible.

Human dependence also grows over time. As AI becomes embedded in daily decisions, workflows adjust around it. People begin to rely on outputs, sometimes without realizing how much their judgment has been shaped. This reliance increases the importance of maintenance. When a system influences habits and routines, changes to its behavior ripple outward.

Long-term commitment means acknowledging this dependency. It requires observing not only technical performance but patterns of use. Are decisions improving? Are overrides increasing? Are unexpected outcomes becoming more frequent? These questions do not disappear after deployment. They become more important.

AI systems also reflect organizational clarity. If objectives shift without recalibration, the system may continue optimizing for outdated goals. This misalignment can persist quietly. Sustained attention ensures that intelligence remains aligned with current priorities rather than past assumptions.

Importantly, commitment does not imply constant overhaul. It means steady stewardship. Regular review. Transparent communication about limitations. Visible ownership of adjustments. These practices maintain trust.

Treating AI as a long-term commitment changes how success is measured. It moves from launch milestones to sustained impact. It recognizes that intelligence is part of an evolving human system.

In real work, responsible AI is less about innovation and more about continuity. It is the willingness to stay engaged after the initial excitement fades. Because intelligence, once integrated, does not remain static. It requires care. And that care defines whether AI remains useful over time.

Short-Term Thinking Breaks AI Systems

AI systems are particularly vulnerable to short-term thinking. When treated as projects with fixed timelines and immediate performance targets, they may appear successful at launch but fragile over time. Intelligence embedded in real work does not thrive under purely short-term incentives. It requires continuity.

Project thinking emphasizes delivery. The goal becomes reaching deployment quickly, demonstrating measurable improvement, and moving on. In the context of AI, this approach can create artificial stability. Early results are highlighted. Limitations are downplayed. The system is declared complete. Yet AI systems are not static tools. Their behavior depends on evolving data, shifting usage patterns, and ongoing human interaction.

Short-term incentives often prioritize visible gains over structural resilience. Teams may optimize outputs to meet immediate expectations rather than strengthen feedback mechanisms. Monitoring may be minimized once initial targets are achieved. Over time, this neglect weakens alignment. The system continues to operate, but its fit with real conditions gradually deteriorates.

AI-specific fragility intensifies this effect. Because outputs are probabilistic, trust depends on consistency across time. When a system is tuned aggressively for early performance, it may lack the stability needed for sustained reliability. Minor changes in inputs or context can produce disproportionate effects. Without long-term oversight, these shifts accumulate.

Trust erosion follows a similar pattern. In early stages, enthusiasm may mask uncertainty. Users tolerate imperfections because improvement feels recent and visible. When attention shifts away and adjustments slow, confidence declines quietly. Small inconsistencies, once acceptable, begin to feel like neglect. The perception that the system is no longer cared for weakens confidence.

Short-term thinking also disrupts responsibility. When ownership is tied to project milestones, accountability may fade after delivery. AI systems, however, continue influencing decisions. If no one remains clearly responsible for observing drift or addressing concerns, misalignment persists unchecked.

Long-term value emerges from steady refinement rather than rapid rollout. This refinement includes reviewing objectives as they evolve, reinforcing boundaries, and maintaining open channels for feedback. These activities may not produce immediate metrics, but they sustain relevance.

Recognizing how short-term incentives undermine AI systems encourages a shift in mindset. Instead of asking only how quickly intelligence can be deployed, organizations must ask how it will be sustained. The fragility of AI does not lie in its complexity alone, but in how it is governed over time.

In real work, intelligence that is introduced quickly but neglected gradually loses credibility. Treating AI as a continuing responsibility rather than a completed project protects both performance and trust. Short-term thinking may deliver early results, but it often compromises the endurance that responsible AI requires.

Learning Never Ends (For Humans Either)

AI systems are often described as learning systems. They adapt to patterns, incorporate feedback, and adjust behavior over time. What is less frequently acknowledged is that organizations must learn alongside them. When intelligence evolves but human understanding remains static, misalignment grows.

AI does not operate in isolation. Its outputs influence decisions, and those decisions reshape processes and expectations. As this cycle continues, both the system and the organization change. Treating learning as something the model does alone overlooks the human side of adaptation.

Human judgment must evolve in response to experience with AI. Early in adoption, people may be cautious. Over time, as familiarity increases, confidence grows. This shift is natural, but it requires reflection. Are users becoming appropriately calibrated in their trust? Are they recognizing the system's boundaries? Without conscious attention, reliance may drift toward either overconfidence or unnecessary skepticism.

Feedback plays a central role in this shared learning. AI systems rely on corrective signals to remain aligned. Humans rely on experience to refine interpretation. When feedback loops are active and visible, both sides adjust constructively. When feedback slows or becomes distorted, learning stalls. The system may adapt in ways users do not understand, and users may change behavior without recognizing the consequences.

Organizations must also revisit objectives. Business priorities shift. Risk tolerance evolves. A system optimized for yesterday's context may no longer align with today's needs. Continuous learning means reassessing whether intelligence still supports the right decisions. It requires openness to recalibration rather than assuming stability.

Evolving judgment is another dimension. As AI becomes embedded in daily work, people develop new skills. They learn to interpret probabilistic outputs, to question recommendations thoughtfully, and to balance efficiency with oversight. This growth does not occur automatically. It develops through exposure, reflection, and dialogue.

Importantly, learning is not a one-time training event. It is an ongoing process shaped by experience. Organizations that recognize this create space for conversation about AI behavior. They encourage reporting of anomalies. They treat unexpected outcomes as opportunities for adjustment rather than embarrassment.

When learning stops, stagnation follows. AI systems may continue operating, but their relevance declines. Human judgment may remain anchored in outdated assumptions. Gradual misalignment becomes visible only after performance deteriorates.

In real work, intelligence and human understanding evolve together. Responsible AI requires both sides to remain attentive. The system adapts to data. People adapt to experience. When this mutual learning is sustained, AI remains aligned with changing reality.

Learning never ends. Not for the system, and not for those who rely on it. And acknowledging this shared evolution is what allows intelligence to remain useful over time.

Stability Comes From Thinking, Not Technology

When organizations seek stability in AI systems, the instinct is often technical. Improve the model. Increase performance. Add safeguards. Refine outputs. While these efforts matter, they do not create lasting stability on their own. Long-term stability depends less on sophistication and more on how clearly people think about decisions, responsibility, and purpose.

AI systems operate within structures shaped by human judgment. If objectives are unclear, the system's behavior will reflect that ambiguity. If decision ownership is diffuse, accountability weakens. If governance is informal, adaptation becomes inconsistent. No amount of technical refinement can compensate for conceptual confusion.

Clarity is the first anchor of stability. When organizations define precisely which decisions AI should influence—and which it should not—they create boundaries. Boundaries reduce unpredictability. They prevent systems from expanding into areas where oversight is insufficient. Clear thinking about purpose stabilizes behavior more effectively than constant adjustment.

Governance provides the second anchor. Stability requires visible stewardship. Someone must monitor patterns, interpret feedback, and address drift. Without structured oversight, AI systems respond to scattered signals. Adaptation becomes reactive rather than deliberate. Governance is not constraint for its own sake; it is the mechanism that maintains alignment over time.

Decision discipline is equally important. AI systems generate outputs, but humans determine how those outputs shape action. When decision processes are consistent and responsibility is explicit, variability decreases. Users understand when to rely on recommendations and when to intervene. This shared understanding prevents overreaction to minor inconsistencies and reduces erosion of trust.

Technical sophistication can enhance performance, but it cannot replace disciplined thinking. A highly advanced system deployed in an environment of unclear objectives will behave unpredictably. A simpler system embedded within clear decision structures often proves more durable.

Stability also requires restraint. Organizations must resist the urge to expand AI influence without revisiting foundational assumptions. Growth that outpaces clarity introduces fragility. Maintaining stability means asking regularly whether the system still aligns with evolving priorities.

Long-term resilience emerges from continuity of attention. Periodic reflection on objectives, boundaries, and responsibility keeps intelligence grounded. This reflection is strategic, not technical. It ensures that adaptation occurs within defined limits rather than drifting into unintended territory.

In real work, stable AI systems are not those that never change. They are those that evolve within coherent structures. Stability is a product of disciplined thinking applied consistently over time. Technology supports this process, but it does not create it.

Clarity, governance, and responsibility form the foundation. When these are strong, AI systems can adapt without destabilizing. When they are weak, even sophisticated intelligence becomes fragile.

Stability comes from how people think about AI, not from how complex the technology becomes. And that thinking determines whether intelligence endures.

The Quiet Work of Stewardship

Once an AI system is deployed and begins influencing real decisions, the visible work appears complete. The launch has happened. The integration is underway. Results are being observed. Yet the most important phase often begins after attention fades. Maintaining AI systems is less about innovation and more about stewardship.

Stewardship is quiet by nature. It does not produce headlines. It rarely involves dramatic improvements. Instead, it consists of regular review, careful observation, and responsible adjustment. For AI systems, this ongoing care is essential because intelligence interacts continuously with changing conditions.

AI-specific stewardship begins with monitoring behavior over time. Outputs that were aligned months ago may shift subtly as inputs evolve. Patterns of use may change. New edge cases may appear. These developments are rarely abrupt. They unfold gradually, which makes them easy to overlook. Stewards must notice these changes before they accumulate into larger problems.

Review is part of this responsibility. Periodic examination of decisions influenced by AI helps ensure alignment with current objectives. Are outcomes improving? Are users overriding more frequently? Are certain contexts producing unexpected results? These questions sustain relevance. Without them, systems may continue operating long after their fit has weakened.

Stewardship also involves maintaining clear ownership. As organizations grow, roles shift. Teams change. Without explicit responsibility for AI oversight, attention disperses. The system may remain active, but no one feels accountable for its evolution. Quiet work means preserving visible ownership even when the system appears stable.

Another dimension of stewardship is communication. When adjustments are made, users should understand why. When limitations become clearer, they should be acknowledged. Transparency reinforces trust. Silence can be interpreted as neglect, especially when users experience inconsistencies.

Importantly, stewardship does not mean constant redesign. It is not about chasing incremental performance gains or introducing new features regularly. Stability often requires restraint.

Responsible stewards resist unnecessary change that may disrupt established trust. They focus on maintaining alignment rather than pursuing novelty.

Human dependence on AI deepens the need for care. As systems become embedded in daily routines, their influence expands quietly. Changes to behavior can ripple outward. Stewardship ensures that these ripples remain controlled and intentional.

In real work, the longevity of AI systems depends less on breakthrough innovation and more on disciplined oversight. The quiet work of stewardship preserves clarity, reinforces responsibility, and sustains trust.

AI does not maintain itself. It requires attention long after the initial excitement has passed. That attention is rarely dramatic, but it is decisive. Because in the absence of stewardship, even capable intelligence gradually loses alignment. And alignment, once lost, is far more difficult to restore than to maintain.

Stewardship is not a one-time correction. It is a recurring discipline.
Objectives must be revisited. Outcomes must be examined. Assumptions must be tested against reality. What appears stable can drift quietly over time. Alignment survives only when review leads to refinement. The process is continuous, even when the system appears calm.

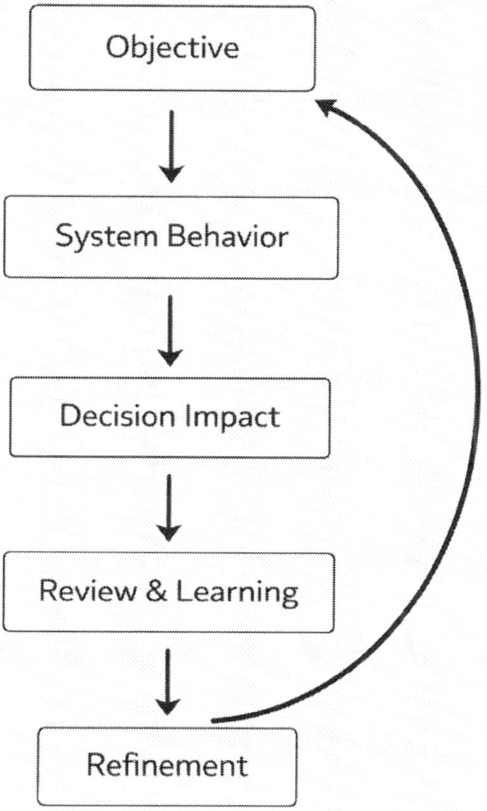

Figure 9. Alignment Is Sustained Through Ongoing Review and Refinement

Avoiding the Next Hype Cycle

Every few years, something new arrives and everyone reacts in almost the same way. The conversation shifts quickly from "Does this help?" to "Why are we not using this yet?" I have watched this pattern repeat across multiple waves of technology. Early success stories circulate. Expectations rise. Leaders feel pressure. Teams rush to experiment. And somewhere in that acceleration, clarity gets lost.

AI makes this cycle even more intense. When AI produces something impressive, it feels intelligent. And when something feels intelligent, we lower our guard. We assume maturity before we have tested stability. That is usually where mistakes begin.

Avoiding the next hype cycle is not about resisting new capability. It is about slowing down your thinking when everyone else speeds up. When something new appears, the first question should not be, "How powerful is this?" The better question is, "What decision does this actually improve?" If you cannot answer that clearly, you are not ready to adopt it. You are reacting to momentum rather than making a deliberate choice.

In my experience, hype compresses critical thinking. Teams begin moving faster than their objectives. Workflows are reorganized around tools before long-term behavior is understood. Demonstrations are optimized instead of outcomes. Anything above zero improvement feels positive, and technically it is. But "above zero" is not a strategy. It is a starting point at best.

Another common mistake is expanding influence too early. A system that performs well in a controlled environment is suddenly positioned as a company-wide solution. Expectations inflate. When reality inevitably introduces complexity, trust erodes. The issue is rarely capability alone. It is misalignment between promise and readiness.

The real protection against hype is discipline. Discipline in defining objectives before adoption. Discipline in setting boundaries. Discipline in preserving human judgment. Discipline in saying, "Not yet," even when external pressure suggests otherwise.

New capabilities will continue to emerge. That is not the problem. The problem is abandoning principles when something looks impressive. If an organization already struggles with unclear ownership or vague objectives, scaling intelligence will not solve those weaknesses. It will magnify them. AI amplifies whatever structure it enters. Strong thinking becomes stronger. Weak thinking becomes visible.

Avoiding the next hype cycle does not require predicting the future. It requires consistency in how change is evaluated. Clear decisions. Defined responsibility. Calibrated trust. Steady stewardship. When these remain intact, new waves of capability become manageable rather than disruptive.

The goal is not to move slower than everyone else. The goal is to move deliberately. In the long run, that difference is what separates maturity from reaction.

What Will Still Matter in Ten Years

Technology will change. Interfaces will improve. Capabilities will expand. Models will become faster, more refined, and more accessible. But if there is one thing experience teaches you, it is this: the fundamentals move far more slowly than the tools.

Ten years from now, organizations will still be making decisions under uncertainty. AI will still produce probabilistic outputs, not certainty. And people will still be responsible for the consequences of those decisions. That structure does not change simply because the systems become more advanced.

Clarity of objectives will still matter. It does not matter how capable a system becomes—if the underlying goal is vague, the output will drift. I have seen this repeatedly. Intelligence amplifies direction. If direction is unclear, amplification only increases confusion. Ten years from now, defining which decision is being improved will remain the starting point.

Ownership will still matter. Someone must stand behind the decision process. AI may inform, recommend, or prioritize, but accountability will remain human. The responsibility gap does not disappear with sophistication. If anything, it becomes more important as systems influence more decisions.

Trust will still matter. And trust will still be built gradually, through consistent behavior over time. There is no shortcut to that. Regardless of how advanced systems become, users will need to understand boundaries, limitations, and patterns of behavior. Confidence will continue to depend on predictability more than raw performance.

Governance will still matter. As AI systems scale, they will require structure around feedback, oversight, and adaptation. This is not about regulation or policy language. It is about stewardship. Systems that influence decisions widely must be monitored deliberately. That principle does not age.

Human judgment will still matter. AI can support reasoning, but it does not replace context. It does not carry accountability. It does not interpret nuance in the same way people do. Organizations that preserve disciplined human oversight will remain more stable than those that attempt to automate judgment entirely.

And perhaps most importantly, thinking will still matter. Clear thinking about decisions. Clear thinking about boundaries. Clear thinking about responsibility. These principles are not tied to a generation of technology. They are structural.

New capabilities will emerge. That is certain. But the organizations that navigate change well will not be those that chase every shift. They will be those that apply the same enduring principles consistently.

In ten years, the vocabulary may change. The tools will certainly evolve. But disciplined thinking about how intelligence influences decisions—that will still matter. And it will likely matter even more.

A Calm Outlook on AI's Future

Conversations about AI often swing between extremes. On one side, it is presented as a transformative force that will solve nearly every problem. On the other, it is described as a destabilizing technology that will undermine judgment and control. In my experience, reality rarely sits at either extreme.

AI will become more embedded in daily work. That is already happening. Systems will assist with analysis, prioritize information, and support routine decisions. But assistance is not the same as autonomy. Most meaningful decisions will continue to involve human judgment, context, and responsibility.

The long-term role of AI is likely to resemble infrastructure rather than spectacle. It will fade into the background of workflows. Instead of being the focus of every meeting, it will become a quiet contributor. People will consult it naturally, much like they consult data or expert opinion today.

Consider a practical example. Imagine a financial review process where managers assess budget allocations across departments. An AI system might surface unusual spending patterns or forecast potential shortfalls based on trends. That support can save time and highlight risks. But the final decision—whether to adjust budgets, reallocate resources, or accept temporary variance—still depends on human priorities and judgment. The AI informs. It does not decide.

This pattern is likely to persist. AI will improve efficiency and visibility. It will reduce friction in information-heavy tasks. But the structure of accountability will remain human. Decisions that affect people, strategy, or risk tolerance will continue to require interpretation beyond statistical patterns.

There will be adjustments. Roles may evolve. Some repetitive analysis may be automated. But the fundamental dynamic—intelligence supporting judgment—will remain steady. Organizations that approach AI with calm discipline rather than fear or hype will adapt more smoothly.

A calm outlook does not mean ignoring risk. It means recognizing that most outcomes are shaped by how systems are designed and governed. With clear objectives, defined responsibility, and steady oversight, AI becomes manageable.

The future of AI in work is neither dramatic salvation nor inevitable disruption. It is gradual integration. It is refinement. It is disciplined use over time.

When viewed this way, the path forward becomes less about reacting to headlines and more about maintaining principles. And that is a far more stable foundation for whatever developments come next.

What This Book Was Really About

If there is one idea I hope stays with you after closing this book, it is this: AI is not about tools. It is about decisions. It is about clarity. It is about how humans choose to think when intelligence enters the room.

Throughout these pages, we have not focused on features or platforms. Those will change. What does not change is the structure of decision-making. Someone defines an objective. Someone evaluates uncertainty. Someone carries responsibility. AI can support that process, but it does not replace it.

In many conversations, I notice a quiet fear underneath the excitement. People wonder whether relying on AI will weaken judgment, or reduce human capability. I see it differently. We have been here before.

There was a time when calculations were done manually. Then calculators arrived. Some worried that mental arithmetic would disappear and that people would become less capable. What actually happened? Repetitive calculations became faster and more accurate. That freed attention for more complex reasoning. We did not become less intelligent. We redirected our intelligence.

The same pattern appeared with computers. Tasks that once consumed hours became manageable in minutes. Did that reduce human capability? No. It expanded what we could attempt. We shifted from mechanical effort to higher-order thinking.

AI fits into that same arc. It can process patterns quickly, highlight anomalies, and assist with repetitive analysis. When used thoughtfully, it does not shrink human judgment. It creates space for deeper questions—strategy, ethics, creativity, and long-term thinking.

But that outcome is not automatic. It depends on how we integrate intelligence into our decisions. If we treat AI as a substitute for clarity, we create confusion. If we treat it as an amplifier of disciplined thinking, we expand our capability.

This book was never about resisting technology. It was about grounding it. It was about reminding ourselves that intelligence—whether human or artificial—needs direction. Clear objectives. Defined ownership. Steady judgment.

AI is a tool, yes. But more importantly, it is a mirror. It reflects the quality of our thinking. If we are careless, it amplifies carelessness. If we are disciplined, it strengthens discipline.

The question was never whether AI will make us less capable. The real question is whether we will use it to elevate the quality of our decisions. And that choice, as it has always been, remains human.

AI Is a Responsibility

If there is one final idea I would leave with you, it is this: AI is not a threat, and it is not a miracle. It is a responsibility.

Intelligence—of any kind—magnifies intent. When used carelessly, it spreads confusion faster. When used thoughtfully, it multiplies clarity and impact. AI does not determine its own direction. We do. That is both the challenge and the opportunity.

Over the years, I have seen technology evolve in waves. Each time, the same question appears beneath the surface: will this replace us, or will it strengthen us? In practice, the outcome depends far less on the technology and far more on how we use it.

AI can process patterns at a scale no individual can match. It can assist with analysis, highlight risks, and surface insights we might overlook. When integrated with discipline, it makes our work faster, sharper, and more informed. It allows us to focus on complex judgment, creative thinking, and long-term strategy—the areas where human intelligence remains essential.

But none of that happens automatically.

Human beings are still more capable than any system we build. We define objectives. We choose boundaries. We interpret context. And we remain accountable for consequences. If AI becomes more powerful, that does not reduce our responsibility. It increases it. We must continue to develop our own clarity, reasoning, and discipline. The smarter our tools become, the more thoughtful we must be.

I am optimistic about what AI can enable. Used wisely, it can improve efficiency, reduce repetitive burden, and support better decisions across industries. It can help us solve problems faster and approach challenges with deeper insight. That is not a distant future—it is already visible.

At the same time, optimism must be paired with caution. Misuse, overconfidence, and neglect can erode trust quickly. That is why stewardship matters. That is why clarity matters. That is why human judgment remains central.

AI is not here to diminish human capability. It is here to extend it—if we choose to handle it well.

The future of AI will not be defined by how advanced the systems become. It will be defined by how responsibly we integrate them into our work and our decisions. If we remain disciplined, thoughtful, and committed to learning, AI can become one of the most constructive tools we have ever built.

The responsibility is ours. And that is a positive thing.

AI will not replace human judgment.
But judgment that refuses to evolve will replace itself.

Decision-First Reflection Notes

1. If a decision does not change, value does not change. AI creates impact only when behavior shifts.
2. A prediction is not an outcome. A decision is the bridge between the two.
3. Accuracy can impress. Changed decisions create results.
4. Clarity is cheaper than optimization. Most complexity is the cost of unclear objectives.
5. Define the decision before designing the system. Everything else follows.
6. Ownership must be clear before intelligence is deployed. Responsibility cannot be automated.
7. A proof of concept proves possibility. Production proves discipline.
8. Scaling multiplies patterns. Strong thinking becomes stronger. Weak thinking becomes visible.
9. Trust grows slowly through consistency and declines quickly through surprise.
10. A highly accurate system that no one trusts will not influence behavior.
11. Automation reduces effort. Augmentation improves judgment. Know which one you are building.

12. More data does not fix unclear decisions. It often amplifies confusion.
13. When objectives are vague, systems become complicated. When objectives are clear, systems become focused.
14. Human judgment does not disappear in AI systems. It shifts location.
15. Feedback is not optional. Without it, learning systems quietly degrade.
16. If no one is accountable for the outcome, the system will eventually be ignored.
17. Saying "not yet" to AI can be a sign of maturity, not resistance.
18. Governance will emerge whether designed or not. It is better to design it.
19. Efficiency is useful. Discipline is essential.
20. AI amplifies intent. It does not correct poor reasoning.
21. The long-term cost of AI is rarely infrastructure. It is stewardship.
22. Trust is contextual. It must be earned within each decision environment.
23. Production systems require clarity about failure, not just success.
24. Human–AI interaction is not a feature. It is the operating model.
25. The smarter our systems become, the more deliberate our thinking must be

Tables

Table 1. Tool-First vs. Decision-First Thinking

Tool-first thinking	Decision-first thinking
Starts with available technology	Starts with the decision that needs improvement
Asks "what can this model do?"	Asks "what decision must change?"
Optimizes performance metrics	Clarifies desired outcomes
Ownership is often unclear	Decision owner is defined early
Focuses on features and capabilities	Focuses on behavior and impact
Treats risk as a technical issue	Treats risk as a decision responsibility issue
Scales technology first	Scales only after decision stability is proven
Seeks impressive demonstrations	Seeks sustained behavioral change
Builds complexity to handle uncertainty	Reduces ambiguity before building
Measures success by system performance	Measures success by decision quality and outcomes
Trust is assumed from accuracy	Trust is earned through consistency
Long-term maintenance is reactive	Long-term stewardship is planned from the start

Table 2. Proof of Concept (POC) vs. Production AI Systems

Proof of Concept (POC)	Production AI System
Controlled and limited environment	Real-world, unpredictable environment
Temporary ownership or shared responsibility	Clearly defined long-term accountability
Stable and curated inputs	Changing, noisy, and incomplete inputs
Trust assumed from demo performance	Trust earned through consistent behavior
Minimal monitoring during test phase	Continuous monitoring and review required
Limited exposure to real consequences	Direct exposure to operational and business risk
Demonstrates technical possibility	Influences real decisions and outcomes
Failure is low-impact and reversible	Failure carries operational or reputational cost
Short-term experimentation mindset	Long-term stewardship mindset
Maintenance is rarely considered	Ongoing maintenance is unavoidable

Table 3. Automation vs. Augmentation in AI

Automation	Augmentation
System executes the decision	Human retains final decision authority
Ownership shifts toward the system's outcome	Ownership remains clearly human
Appropriate when risk is bounded and predictable	Appropriate when judgment and context matter
Reduces human involvement in routine tasks	Supports and enhances human judgment
Failure impact can scale quickly if unchecked	Failure is often moderated by human oversight
Trust must be strong before deployment	Trust builds gradually through collaboration
Best suited for repetitive, stable decisions	Best suited for complex or contextual decisions
Emphasizes efficiency and consistency	Emphasizes decision quality and understanding

Table 4. Signals That AI May Not Be the Right Solution

Signal	Why It Matters
The objective is unclear or constantly changing	AI will amplify ambiguity and produce inconsistent outcomes
No clear decision owner is defined	Without accountability, the system will lack oversight and trust
The decision has high ethical or moral sensitivity	Human judgment and contextual reasoning may be essential
There is no reliable feedback loop	The system cannot adapt or correct itself over time
The decision occurs rarely	Limited repetition reduces learning value and justification for automation
Risk is high and human oversight is absent	Small errors can create disproportionate consequences
Trust in the process is already weak	AI may deepen skepticism rather than improve confidence
The problem is procedural, not analytical	Process redesign may solve the issue without adding intelligence
Data quality is inconsistent and unmanaged	Poor inputs will produce unstable behavior
The organization lacks long-term stewardship capacity	AI requires ongoing review, not one-time deployment

Table 5A. AI Maturity Levels and Structural Characteristics

Level	Focus	Ownership	Trust Pattern
Curiosity	Exploring AI possibilities	Unclear or loosely shared	Hype-driven
Experimentation	Running pilots and POCs	Technical teams	Conditional, fragile
Operationalization	Deploying in limited scope	Defined owner	Cautious, monitored
Integration	Embedding in workflows	Business owner with oversight	Contextual trust
Stewardship	Long-term responsibility	Explicit governance structure	Calibrated, stable

Table 5B. Risk Patterns, Common Mistakes, and What Improves

Level	Risk Pattern	Typical Mistake	What Improves
Curiosity	Underestimated	Confusing demos with value	Awareness
Experimentation	Localized	Avoiding production accountability	Learning speed
Operationalization	Process friction	Overconfidence in early success	Reliability
Integration	Cross-team misalignment	Scaling without clarity	Consistency
Stewardship	Managed and visible	Neglecting maintenance	Sustainable impact

Appendix

AI Evaluation Checklist

Before implementing or scaling any AI system, leaders and teams should pause and ask the following questions. These are not technical questions. They are discipline questions.

1. What specific decision will this AI system improve or influence?

2. If this system performs well, what behavior will change in practice?

3. Who is the clearly defined owner of the decision this system affects?

4. Who remains accountable if the system produces an incorrect or harmful outcome?

5. Is the objective stable, measurable, and understood across teams?

6. What happens when the system fails? Is that consequence acceptable?

7. How will trust be earned and maintained over time?

8. Is this initiative automation or augmentation? Have we chosen intentionally?

9. Do we have a reliable feedback loop to review and refine system behavior?

10. Are we prepared to monitor this system continuously once deployed?

11. What will scaling this system amplify—strength or misalignment?

12. Does the organization have the discipline and capacity for long-term stewardship?

13. Are we introducing AI to solve a decision problem—or to compensate for unclear processes?

14. Is human judgment positioned appropriately within the system?

15. If we decided not to use AI here, what alternative would we pursue?

How to Use This Checklist

This checklist is not meant to slow innovation. It is meant to protect clarity.

Use it before approving a new AI initiative, before moving from proof of concept to production, and before scaling an existing system. The goal is not to answer every question perfectly. The goal is to expose assumptions early.

If several questions cannot be answered clearly, the issue is rarely technical. It is usually conceptual. That is the moment to pause, refine objectives, and define ownership.

AI systems perform best when the thinking around them is disciplined. This checklist is a tool for maintaining that discipline over time.

How to Use This Book

This book is structured around principles rather than tools. You do not need to read it strictly from beginning to end, although doing so will provide a complete framework. Depending on your role, certain sections may be immediately more relevant.

Business leaders should begin with the chapters on decisions, objectives, and trust. These sections clarify why AI initiatives often fail before technical work begins and how decision ownership shapes outcomes. Understanding these foundations will help you evaluate proposals more effectively and set realistic expectations.

Technical professionals may benefit from starting with the chapters on architecture, production realities, and human–AI interaction. These sections explore how clarity influences system design, how scaling changes behavior, and why long-term stewardship matters as much as model performance.

Product teams should focus on the chapters discussing objectives, proof of concept versus production, and feedback loops. These areas provide guidance on translating ambition into sustainable systems and avoiding the common trap of demo-driven progress.

Executives considering AI adoption may find it helpful to begin with the chapters on when not to use AI and on scaling responsibly. These sections encourage disciplined thinking before committing significant resources and highlight the importance of governance and accountability.

Consultants and advisors can use the comparison tables, evaluation checklist, and reflection notes as practical tools. These sections provide structured ways to facilitate discussions, assess readiness, and frame AI initiatives around decision impact rather than technology alone.

While each chapter stands on its own, the central theme remains consistent: AI creates value when it improves decisions. Use this book as a guide to think more clearly, ask better questions, and approach AI with both confidence and discipline.

Glossary (Plain English)

Decision

A choice that leads to action. In the context of AI, value is created only when a system influences or improves a real decision. Without a decision, outputs remain information.

Prediction

An estimate about what is likely to happen. AI systems often generate predictions, but predictions alone do not create impact until someone acts on them.

Drift

The gradual change in how a system performs because real-world conditions evolve. Over time, data patterns shift, and a once-reliable system may behave differently unless reviewed and adjusted.

Feedback Loop

A structured way of reviewing outcomes and feeding that learning back into the system. In AI, feedback allows systems and teams to correct errors and improve performance over time.

Automation

Using AI to execute a decision with little or no human involvement. Automation is most appropriate when decisions are repetitive, stable, and low-risk.

Augmentation
Using AI to support human judgment rather than replace it. The human remains the final decision-maker, and the system enhances clarity or speed.

Stewardship
The ongoing responsibility of maintaining and reviewing an AI system after deployment. Stewardship includes monitoring behavior, managing risk, and ensuring the system continues to serve its intended purpose.

Governance
The structure of roles, responsibilities, and rules surrounding AI use. Governance clarifies who owns decisions, who reviews outcomes, and how risk is managed.

Trust Calibration
Aligning human confidence in a system with its actual reliability. Over-trust and under-trust both reduce value; the goal is informed, balanced reliance.

Objective Clarity
A clear understanding of what the system is meant to improve. When objectives are precise, systems remain focused. When objectives are vague, complexity increases.

Scaling
Expanding an AI system beyond its original environment or user group. Scaling amplifies both strengths and weaknesses, making discipline more important.

Model Behavior
How an AI system responds to different inputs over time. Behavior includes not just accuracy, but consistency, stability, and predictability.

Accountability
Clear responsibility for decisions and outcomes influenced by AI. Even when systems provide recommendations, accountability remains human.

Human Oversight
Active monitoring and review by people to ensure AI systems operate as intended. Oversight helps detect drift, errors, or unintended consequences.

Production Environment
The real-world setting where an AI system influences actual decisions. Unlike controlled tests, production environments include uncertainty and changing conditions.

Proof of Concept (POC)
A limited experiment designed to demonstrate feasibility. A POC shows what is possible, but it does not prove long-term reliability or readiness.

Decision Owner
The individual or role responsible for the final outcome of a decision influenced by AI. Clear ownership reduces confusion and improves trust.

Operational Risk
The potential negative consequences that arise when an AI system fails or behaves unexpectedly in real work settings.

Consistency
The ability of an AI system to behave predictably over time. Consistency builds trust more effectively than occasional impressive results.

Augmented Judgment
A decision-making approach where human reasoning is

supported by AI insights. The system informs; the human decides.

Acknowledgments

No meaningful work is created in isolation.

Over the years, I have had the privilege of working with colleagues, clients, mentors, and teams across different countries and industries. Many of the ideas in this book were shaped not in quiet reflection alone, but in real conversations—during architecture reviews, project discussions, production challenges, and thoughtful debates about how intelligence should be applied responsibly.

I am grateful to the teams who trusted me to work alongside them in complex AI initiatives. The lessons learned through real implementation—successes and setbacks alike—have influenced the thinking behind these pages.

I would also like to acknowledge the broader technology community. The culture of open knowledge sharing within the Python and AI ecosystem continues to inspire disciplined thinking and collaborative growth.

Finally, to those who encourage thoughtful work over rushed output—your belief in clarity over noise has mattered more than you know.

This book is the result of many interactions, shared ideas, and collective learning over time.

Thank you.

About the Author

Saurabh Jaiswal works at the intersection of software engineering, artificial intelligence, and disciplined thinking.

Over the past fifteen years, he has built systems in Python and data-driven environments across industries including banking, healthcare, research, and cloud platforms. For more than five years, his work has focused specifically on applied artificial intelligence—helping organizations move from experimentation to responsible, production-ready AI systems.

Across different countries and organizational cultures, he has observed a consistent pattern: technology evolves quickly, but clarity often does not. Many AI initiatives struggle not because of weak engineering, but because of unclear decisions, undefined ownership, or misplaced expectations. That observation shaped his decision-first philosophy.

Rather than beginning with tools or trends, Saurabh begins with the question: What decision are we trying to improve? He believes intelligence only creates value when it changes real behavior—and that responsibility does not disappear when systems become smarter.

Colleagues describe him as thoughtful, energetic, and grounded. He combines optimism about AI's potential with steady realism about risk, trust, and long-term stewardship. His work emphasizes clarity over complexity, discipline over hype, and sustainable impact over short-term excitement.

Based in Belgium and collaborating with global teams, Saurabh continues to write, teach, and advise on building AI systems that are not only intelligent—but trusted, aligned, and practical in real work.

Technology moves fast. Thinking should remain disciplined.

AI cannot replace humans — but humans who use AI thoughtfully will always move ahead.

Stay Connected

If this book helped you think more clearly about AI, decisions, and responsible adoption, the conversation continues.

I share reflections, practical frameworks, and long-term thinking on disciplined AI at:

Personal Website: www.saurabhjaiswal.com

Additional writing and learning resources:

Blogs: www.blogmates.org
Tutorials: www.pythonmates.com

Thank you for investing your time and attention in this book.

Continue building. Continue questioning. Continue thinking clearly.

Made in United States
Troutdale, OR
11/03/2026

56845394R00126